The Enchanted World

GODS AND GODDESSES

The Enchanted World

GODS AND GODDESSES

by the Editors of Time-Life Books

The Content

Time-Life Books · Alexandria, Virginia

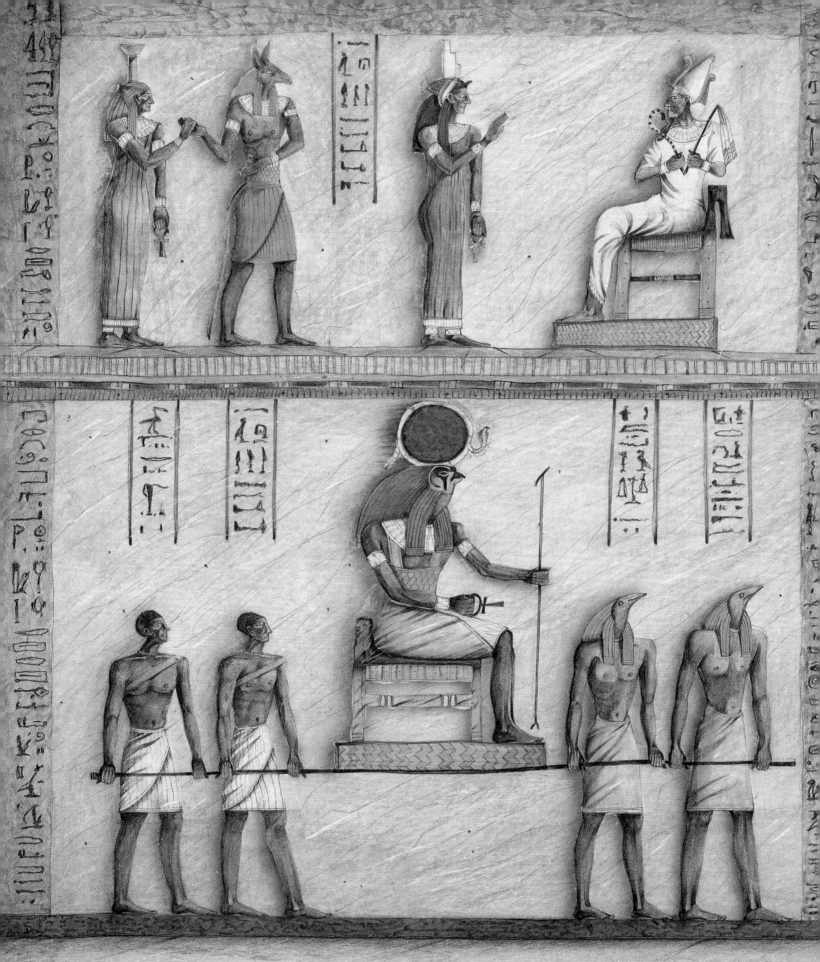

Divinities of preternatural wisdom and awesome powers, the gods and goddesses of
Egypt were depicted sometimes in human form, sometimes with the heads of the beasts
and birds that were their mystical symbols: jackals, lions, ibis and other creatures
that dwelled in the desert and on the verges of the Nile.

One

God-Kings of the Nile

There was at time's beginning a land whose Kings were gods. This was Egypt, womb of magic and birthplace of the sun. In every generation, its Pharaoh was a deity, the scion of a dynasty that began at the Creation. He was the lineal descendant and literal incarnation of Ra, the solar patriarch, of falcon-eyed Horus, and of Osiris, lord of the underworld. His subjects hailed him as the source of all life, shepherd of the land, guardian of the harvests, controller of the Nile. Under his hand, Egypt flourished.

In an Empire so blessed, great things were possible. Priestly scribes dipped reed brushes into paint to record the conquest of the Sea People, the Hittites and the men of Kush. On the towering columns of the magnificent temples at Luxor and Karnak, sculptors lauded their rulers in stone. By the light of oil lamps, artists limned their lords' life histories and glories on the inner walls of burial chambers. This they did for the enlightenment of the departed, whose winged souls would emerge each night through the false doors drawn on their coffins, to read the papyrus scrolls set out for them.

In this land, mortality held no terrors, for its god-kings had conquered death, and made eternity a part of Egypt. The first of these royal divinities, forefather and creator of all things, was Ra, lord of the sun. He was the patriarch of a large and many-branched clan of gods. In a shining ship that some called the Barque of Millions of Years, he daily sailed across the sky; in a second craft, serpent-prowed and crewed by stars, he navigated by night the dark waters of the underworld.

But the day came when Ra, in his palace on the hill of Heliopolis, grew angry. A sound that had seemed at first as irritating and insignificant as the buzzing of flies resolved itself into the voices of his human subjects, raised in complaint.

The light Ra sent them, they said, was too hot. The fierce noon rays turned the skin of their backs to stiff, cracking leather. Furthermore, he let the red orb rise too early in the mornings, when weary laborers still longed for sleep. Then he took it away at night, when they were most in need of it, leaving them vulnerable to the jackals, snakes and other predators of the darkness.

The heat of Ra's sun was powerful indeed, but it was nothing to the white-hot anger aroused by this ingratitude. Ra stood before the gold-tipped granite shaft at the center of his citadel, looking down at the world he had made.

To the west, the broad Nile was in full spate, bringing life to the soil and wealth to the farmer. Ra looked north to the canals, islands and flood plains of the river delta. Through the bulrushes he saw the white-sailed barges plying the waterway, saw the fig trees, date palms and acacias that lined its banks. To the south he perceived a human anthill of slave laborers at work in the necropolis, hauling tubs of mortar and baskets of bricks to build some great man's tomb. Finally, he looked beyond the long ribbon of green to the bleached-out seas of sand, and thought how little his people knew of his true power. He had given his life for them, drained his own vital sources to animate their limbs, and they had the temerity to speak against him. With a roar of disgust, Ra wrenched one of his eyes from its socket and hurled it at his creation.

Oblivious to the pain of this self-mutilation—indeed, some sages claimed that the god's eye was a separate, living entity with a will of its own—Ra watched the glowing orb cleave the air. Far below him, he saw the faces of ungrateful humankind contort with horror. The eye, mid-flight, had shifted its shape and become a goddess bent on destruction.

Her name, the chroniclers said later, was Sekhmet, and she came to take revenge. She struck out in all directions. Maddened by her thirst for blood, she sucked the living juices from her victims and left their dry husks littering the riverbanks, lying facedown in the wadis, and blowing across the desert sands. Humankind faced extinction.

Confronted with this catastrophe, Ra repented of his anger. He had wished to punish his children, not destroy them. But Sekhmet was running amok. The sun-god devised a ruse to stop her. Know-

ing that she was avid for more blood, he brewed a potent beer from red barley. Then he mixed it with a powder made from mandrakes, the roots of forked and human shape that shrieked when torn from the earth. The resulting liquid looked and smelled like human blood. He poured a great quantity of it onto the ground, creating a flood of gore that Sekhmet could hardly fail to see as she moved across Egypt in her path of destruction. She stopped before the scarlet lake, sniffed curiously, then drained every drop of the liquid. She launched forth once again on her hunt for new victims, then staggered as the brew knocked her off balance.

Within minutes, she was fast asleep. When she woke, her head was sore but her mood was milder, and humankind was, thanks to Ra's intervention, spared further destruction.

For Ra, curbing Sekhmet was a relatively simple accomplishment. He was used to confronting monsters far more ghastly. Every day, as he sailed his solar barque along the celestial counterpart of the earthly Nile, a massive serpent rose up from the depths. This was Apep, Ra's old adversary. Inevitably, the great snake of darkness opened his mouth to engulf the vessel. Sometimes Apep's attempts were very nearly successful, and then the world would be battered by dreadful storms, or plunged into an eclipse. But Ra used all his magical resources to defeat the beast. Some accounts said that he de-

humiliated the scaly masters of the underworld by forcing them to draw his barque through the waters as if they were beasts of burden. Small wonder then that Ra turned bitter when faced with the thanklessness of his human subjects. He withdrew from Heliopolis to dwell in heaven. Soon he felt himself growing old and tired. His mind wandered and his conversation with it. In his great white mansion, servants scurried back and forth in obedience to his increasingly contradictory commands. Ra's children and grandchildren, gods and goddesses themselves, laughed behind their hands. The old King still held the ankh, the looped cross that was the key of life and symbol of royal power, but the younger members of his household chafed against his caprices and irrational demands.

Yet one of Ra's family, the goddess Isis, took no part in such rebellious murmurings. True, she recoiled from the old King's yellow fingers when he sought to greet her in a great-grandfatherly embrace, and she averted her eyes when he hobbled, propped up by attendants, to and from the barques of day and night.

...flected the scaly monster by whispering unknown but fearful words of awesome power. Others told how he transformed himself into a great clawed cat from the jungles in the south, to lash out at the wedge-shaped head and the eyes that glittered a message of menace.

Ra encountered other enemies on his nightly voyages, as he sailed his barque through the underworld's twelve provinces to bring a glimmer of light to the human dead. Each of these realms was governed by a snake unlike any found on earth. In one district, a two-headed serpent governed. Another was ruled by a reptile with four bearded human heads growing out of its back, lurching and bobbing as the creature moved.

These kings of the dead were vampires, hungry not for human blood but for human spirits. Had it not been for the eye of Ra upon them, they would have gorged themselves on the souls in their care. When Ra's barque sailed along this Nile of night, demons danced on the banks of the river, hissing poison. But the lord of the sun subdued them all, and

For Isis, the power plays and court gossip of her relations held little interest. She was a solitary, who kept her own counsel. Her family left her to herself, and this suited her purposes.

She spent her days far from the turquoise and marble halls of the royal house, in wild, lonely places unmarked on any map. There, away from prying eyes and the ears of palace spies, she

By day, Ra rode the skies in his sun barque, illumining the earth. At night he descended, in another craft, to ply the dark waters of death's kingdom.

conferred with priestesses of wild and alien aspect. Together they devised and perfected the arts of sorcery.

Isis learned how to inscribe amulets with words of power, how to draw magic circles with a wand of hippopotamus ivory, how to exploit the special potencies of scorpions, crocodiles and oryx gazelles by engraving their images on smooth-faced stones. She could cast her eye through days and seasons still to come, to mark times of good and evil omen, and it was easy for her to slip inside the souls of sleepers and read or alter the messages encoded within their dreams.

She gathered up an arsenal of skills and subtleties. When the time was right, she used them to bend aged Ra, the ever weakening reed, to the hot wind of her will. In his infirmity, the old King had begun to drool and slaver, a matter of great repulsion to the smooth-skinned, sweet-breathed children of his house. But as they began to shun the old god's company, Isis grew more attentive. She made sure that his every need was met, helped him to food and drink, and used the linen of her own finespun garments to wipe the spittle from his wet lips. Patiently she collected this saliva, each night wringing out the liquid from her gown with tightly clenched fists.

One night, when she had gathered up what she deemed a sufficient quantity, she used her gifts as maker and magician to form a viper from the slime and drool, and gave it life. On the following morning, when Ra went down to the river, the serpent of Isis slid across his path and buried its fangs in his flesh.

As fast as rumor, the poison spread throughout his body. He sweated and shivered, babbling incomprehensible, arcane secrets in his delirium. Creator though he was, this reptile was not of Ra's own making. Without knowing its secret name and its innermost essence, even he, greatest of the gods, was powerless to confect an antidote. As the venom bubbled in his veins, his howls could be heard in Sumer, in Syria, and in the far kingdom of Kush, as well as in the twelve regions of the underworld.

The royal family gathered about their fallen patriarch. Gods and goddesses they might be, but they had no way to help him, and the distress on their faces was deep and unfeigned.

Then Isis rose up in the midst of the multitude, cleared her throat and announced that she might—just might—know a cure. But her magic would not work with so many witnesses. The rest of the household withdrew, leaving Ra on the ground where he had fallen, his back arched in agony.

Isis kneeled beside him, gazing down into his pain-dazzled eyes. She knew a certain remedy, she admitted softly, for this particular venomous worm had been of her own making. But for the healing spell to be efficacious, she would need to learn the sun-god's secret name.

Ra's eyes widened in horror. No request in the world could have been more outrageous. Better for a King's nakedness to be seen by strangers than for anyone, even his own flesh and blood, to learn his

Isis and Osiris, her brother as well as her spouse, reigned together after
Ra retired to the heavens. Under their dominion, Egypt flourished,
for they taught its people all the skills and arts of survival.

innermost hidden name—the word behind all words, that had coalesced from
roaring chaos at the birth of the universe.
It was the essence of his spirit and his god-
head, the key that unlocked his power.

Even in his agony, Ra hesitated. Isis
smiled down at him. Then his hands and
feet began to swell, came near to bursting, and his face filled with flame. He
struggled to lift his head. Isis lowered
hers. With a cracked, blackened tongue,
Ra pronounced the sacred syllables.

For one moment, a silence as deep as
death fell upon Creation. The flies
stopped humming and hung motionless in
the air. The Nile seemed for an instant to
pause in its flow. Down in the tombs, the
bandaged dead tossed and murmured inside
their painted sarcophagi. Something had
changed in the order of the universe.

Then Isis reached out her hand and
kept her promise. She sang a spell so potent that no scribe would ever have dared
to write it for posterity. Then she produced a tiny vial of glass as blue as
heaven and anointed Ra with droplets of
the essence it contained.

Soon the sun-god rose up whole again,
though severely shaken. According to
some chroniclers, the rule of the earth
quickly passed to the enchantress Isis and
her consort Osiris who, in the manner of
Egypt's ancient Kings, was her brother as
well as her spouse. They formed a perfect
partnership: Isis, mother-goddess and magician, mistress of the arts of weaving
spells as well as cloth; Osiris, the god of
corn and rich harvests, teacher of the arts

of farming and the skills of survival.

The Sorceress Queen, who had used her occult knowledge to seize power from Ra, now employed this same wisdom to protect and nurture her people. While Isis governed, Osiris journeyed throughout Egypt, spreading the mysteries of agriculture. He taught the people how the annual flooding of the Nile nourished their parched land and controlled the seasons of planting and reaping. With his help, they learned to read the river, to measure the depth of the yearly flood and know the quality of harvest it presaged. Osiris instructed them also in the making of tools, the digging of canals to irrigate the land in the dry times, the use of oxen and the plow, the cultivation of barley, wheat and flax.

Once he had brought these gifts to his people, Osiris left Egypt to confer these same benefits on the uncharted lands beyond. The places he visited and the distances he traveled were not recorded, but signs of his presence and symbols of his worship were to be found wherever people gave up the wandering life of hunters and shepherds, and learned to bring forth sustenance from the earth.

It might be hoped that such a beneficent reign would last forever. But not even the gardens of the gods were free from scorpions. A pair of envious eyes watched Isis and Osiris. A will as strong as theirs worked in secret to do them harm.

The enemy was a member of their own royal family, with the blood of Ra flowing in his veins. His name was Set, patron of mayhem, war and natural disasters. He loved the sound of tearing flesh; the wolf and the jackal were his creatures. Though he was brother to Osiris, most beautiful of the gods, Set himself displayed an alien ugliness. His skin was an unhealthy white, in stark contrast to the warm honey and ebony tones of his brethren, and his hair was a startling red, the color of evil.

According to some chroniclers, Set served Osiris by governing as his viceroy in the hot lands of the south, and chafed because he felt that he, not his sibling, should be the universal ruler. Of all the ancient tales of brother hating brother, Set's was most terrible. He had at his disposal all the powers of godhood, and used them with the cold cunning of a thief who slips through alleys to cut throats as readily as purses.

From birth, Set had been ruthless. It was said that when he waxed impatient in his mother's womb, he ripped and clawed his way to freedom. But as he grew, he learned the art of dissembling, and discovered that a honeyed tongue could be as efficacious as a dagger.

It was probable that Osiris remained unaware of his brother's hatred, for when the corn-god returned from his wanderings, he accepted without hesitation Set's invitation to a feast. The chronicles did not say if Isis accompanied her consort to this banquet, but if she, the mother of magic, had been present, it is unlikely that the tragic events of that day would have been allowed to take their course.

As Osiris headed upstream to the riverside palace of Set, his brother stood waiting on the steps of the landing place to greet him. Slipping a garland of lotus blossoms around his royal brother's neck, the host led his guest of honor to the columned banqueting hall in which six dozen revelers were already assembled.

A serving-maid gave Osiris a cone of perfumed pomade to wear on his head; in the heat of the feast, it would melt down to a sticky glaze, saturating his wig and garments with floral scents. Other attendants, bearing trays of fish, roasted fowl, ripe figs and honey cakes, threaded their way through the swaying dancers. Harpists, flautists, lute players and singers strove to make themselves heard over the din of laughter, gossip, vows of eternal friendship and the clattering of plates and wine cups.

Once Set had satisfied himself that his guests were replete with the delights from his kitchen and vineyard, he signaled to the musicians and demanded silence. He proposed to offer his guests a diversion somewhat out of the ordinary: a competition for a prize worth having.

At Set's nod, four stout servants carried a coffin of extraordinary beauty into the hall. The merrymakers were all wealthy connoisseurs of craftsmanship; they spent fortunes to furnish the tombs in which they anticipated dwelling throughout the afterlife, and whole villages of painters and artisans prospered in the execution of these patrons' commissions. Jostling and murmuring, they admired the coffin's elegant lines, fine veneer and multicolored inlays of ivory and precious stones.

At a feast held by Set, Osiris' envious brother, the host offered a splendid casket as a prize to any guest who fitted its dimensions. Unbeknown to Osiris, the coffin—built secretly to his own measurements—was a lethal trap.

Imprisoned in his own sarcophagus, Osiris was set adrift
by Set to die in the River Nile. The corn-god's coffin was
caught by the current and borne swiftly away from Egypt.

This wonderful article, announced the host, was a gift to anyone whose physical dimensions exactly matched the coffer's capacity. One by one, the tipsy guests attempted to lie down in the empty box. Some were so fat that they could barely fit a single leg into the space; others were so short that two could have lain there together, end to end.

Finally, Osiris himself was persuaded to try for the treasure. If he was amazed to find he filled the box perfectly, he was the only one thus surprised: The chest had been designed by his brother to fit him exactly, and the seventy-two guests who had come to honor Osiris were all conspirators loyal to Set.

With a bang Set slammed down the lid on his brother. A confederate rushed up with a pot of molten metal to seal fast the lid. The servants who had brought in the prize now carried it out again, and Set followed them to the banks of the river. He stood on the same steps where he had first greeted his royal brother, and watched as he departed in very different circumstances. When the coffin had finally disappeared from view, he signaled to his musicians to strike up another tune.

It was not recorded how news of the event came to Isis. A mortal messenger, perhaps a boatman from the god's own barge, or a disgruntled servant escaping from Set's palace, may have brought the word, trembling with horror at the scene he had witnessed, and fearing the great goddess's fury. Or it may have been Isis' own perception of disaster that woke her, shrieking, from her dreams.

She did not waste time in lamentation. At her behest, a silence fell upon the land, that she might listen for the beating of her lover's heart. But she could hear nothing; neither spell nor any other tool of divination gave her sight of him. The river that brought sustenance to the people of Egypt had embraced the god of that nourishment in its inexorable flow and carried him far away.

Just as any devoted earthly wife might go in search of a husband who had vanished under mysterious circumstances, so Isis went into the world to search for Osiris. She was as resolute as the widows who fought off vultures while they combed the corpse-heaps on the

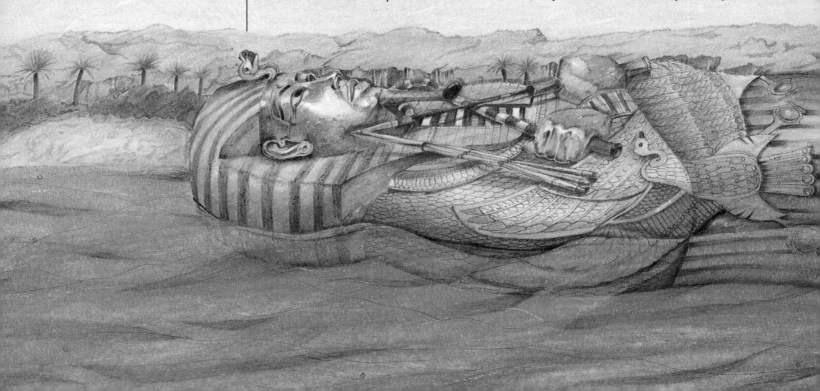

battlefields for their menfolk's broken bodies. She was as patient as those who walked barefoot from one town to the next, scanning the faces of the prisoners in the slave markets.

She followed the river on its journey toward the sea, and when it divided into the numberless streams of the great delta, she stood at the point where the waters diverged, and wept. Suddenly, the goddess was aware of a fragrance wafting on the breeze, far sweeter than any of the perfumes from the land of Punt, or the pounded essences of sweet flag, cassia and convolvulus that so delighted the gods. Isis knew that this was a sign of her beloved. Disguising herself as a humble traveler, she followed the sweet scent northward toward its source, and in so doing, she left the land of Egypt.

Never did Isis speak of the travails of that long journey. Only one event had any meaning for her, and that was her arrival at the port of Byblos, in the great seafaring kingdom of Phoenicia. Here she knew that she had reached the place where the body of Osiris lay hidden.

The fragrance that had led her all the way from Egypt grew ever more intense.

Even the salt and seaweed tang of the harbor did nothing to disguise it. It overshadowed the grassy sweetness of packed papyrus, and the aromas of cut cedarwood, oils and spices that emanated from the holds and decks of the great galleys: cargo ships destined for all the cities along the Great Sea's shores, and for those wild lands beyond the rocky pillars that marked the end of the known world.

Oblivious to the jostling crowds of tattooed seafarers, cursing mule drivers and traders hawking cheap temptations, Isis moved like a ghost through the streets of the city. Then she came to the palace, newly built for the King of that place, Malcandre, and his Queen. The whitest marbles, the most radiant porphyry, had been used in its construction. The finest, fairest trees had been taken from sacred groves and virgin forests to form the pillars holding up its roof. One of these supports was a tamarisk tree, emanating that indefinable and piercing sweetness that had beckoned to Isis from so far away. Within its bark, she knew, lay the coffin of Osiris.

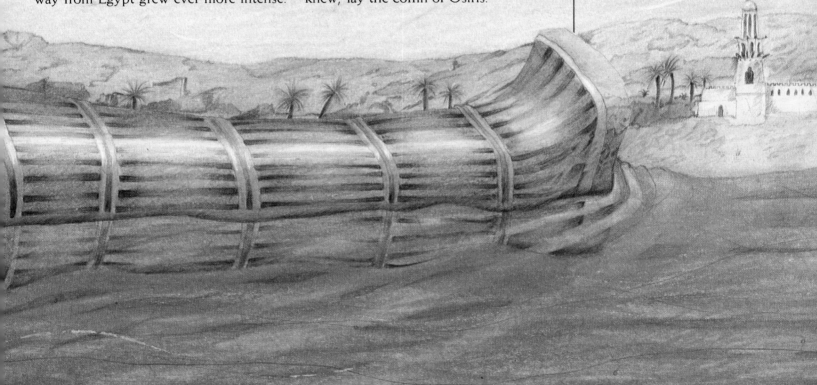

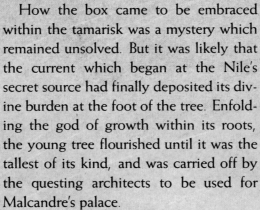

How the box came to be embraced within the tamarisk was a mystery which remained unsolved. But it was likely that the current which began at the Nile's secret source had finally deposited its divine burden at the foot of the tree. Enfolding the god of growth within its roots, the young tree flourished until it was the tallest of its kind, and was carried off by the questing architects to be used for Malcandre's palace.

When Isis revealed herself to the King and Queen, they showed her every kindness. Immediately dispatching workmen to the forest to procure a replacement for the tamarisk pillar, they gave the portion of the tree containing the coffin to Isis. Only then, when her quest was at an end, did she give way to her grief. She wept as copiously as the Nile in fullest flood over the coffin containing the lifeless but still uncorrupted body of Osiris. So moved by her anguish were they that the rulers of Byblos gave her a retinue of guards and servants and a well-provisioned, new-built ship, that she might convey her husband's sarcophagus back to Egypt.

Word of her grim discovery preceded Isis home. When she reached her own country, the land was silent and somber, as if each grain of desert sand and droplet of river water were weighed down by grief. Yet, as the galley of Isis moved upstream, bearing the battered but still beautiful box that had carried Osiris to his doom, the widow herself was fully occupied in a struggle to bring her spouse back to life again. Once more,

the goddess enveloped herself in the mantle of hidden wisdoms that she had worn when she wrested the rule of the world itself from the faltering grasp of the aged Ra. She hunted for the winged soul of her loved one through the swamps and marshes of the underworld. In every cry of the night birds hiding in the reeds she called to him. In every gliding movement of the snakes she sought his spirit. Wielding words of formidable power, she kindled a single spark of the corn-god's vital force from some unknown place and planted it within her womb. Osiris might be dead, but Isis now rejoiced, for she carried his child. Knowing the dangers that loomed over her offspring's head even before he saw the light of day, Isis withdrew to a secret place, fenced in by magic, to bear the babe.

The child was born an orphan, but there was no doubting the divine paternity of the infant Horus. He glowed with godhood. Once his miraculous birth had been accomplished, his mother Isis began the long and painstaking process of luring her lost mate Osiris back to the land of the living. She knew that to achieve this, each of the nine parts that made up his sacred self would have to be restored: his corporeal body, his spiritual body, his world soul, his spirit soul, his shadow, his heart, his life force, his essence and his hidden name.

To do this work in secrecy and safety, Isis concealed her husband's coffin within the marshes along the Nile. She went

Isis searched the world for her mate and found his body in the land of Phoenicia, encased in the bark of a tamarisk tree. Conquering her grief, she wielded her divine powers to bring him back to life.

forth to comb the earth for the herbs and amulets, the sacred stones and elixirs, the holy vessels and books of spells she would need for this enterprise.

But the river was full of crocodiles, and some of them were spies of Set. Word of the coffin's whereabouts went out to this jealous god, and barely had Isis departed on her quest when Set stood over his brother's body, wielding the knife that hunters used to gut and flay.

When Isis came back with the medicines of resurrection, the corn-god's corpse was missing. Perhaps her eye was caught by some small, pale object floating like a water lily among the reeds, or by a stray splinter of bone that snapped beneath her sandal on the shore. When the truth came home to her, she received it impassively and at once began the search for her consort's remains. No matter how many pieces Set had cut the body into, she swore to find them. This, not vengeance, was her first concern. Revenge against Set would be the birthright and mission of Horus, posthumous child of the lost god.

Isis was not alone in her quest. Her sister Nepthys, friend and protectress of the dead, and unloving wife of Set himself, used her own divine powers to help in the hunt for the scattered fragments.

The search for the god's remains took them all over Egypt. It was said by the chroniclers that Set had hewn his brother into fourteen pieces, and that thirteen of these, all but his organs of generation, were ultimately recovered. Yet here the accounts diverged. According to the ancient records, parts of his body were found as far south as Nubia, others in the great necropolis at Abydos and in the lakeland of Fayum. There were forty-two provinces of Egypt, and in every one of them the inhabitants claimed to have found some piece or relic of the god. To this mystery there was no answer.

Once recovered, the body of the god was brought to a place of safety where Isis, ever vigilant, remained. Then the solemn work began that would be the model for all those who studied the arts of mummification and sought the secret of giving flesh eternal life. His limbs were washed in cedar oil and cinnamon, and wrapped in shrouds of finest linen. His entrails were placed in jars of alabaster and preserved with the sacred herb am-

Weary of his sufferings at the hand of Set, Osiris chose to descend to the underworld. There he ruled, as Pharaoh, in the realm of the dead.

sety that some call dill. Then, once more, Isis strained every sinew of her own flesh and spirit to work the magic that would make Osiris whole.

Her struggle filled the land with signs and portents. The dreams of priests and sorcerers were dense with messages. In a temple cut from living rock, in the heart of a valley known to no one, Isis intoned the final words of a spell so terrible that even to describe it would have shattered the universe. The whole of Egypt held its breath, and time, for an instant, stood suspended. Then, just as the Nile flooded the parched land, so joy coursed through every heart. The warm earth stirred and the sky was filled once more with light. Osiris lived again.

And in the moment that Osiris rose, the shoots of all green, growing things stirred to life deep in the soil of Egypt. For, as Isis knew and priests ever after remembered, the corn-god's death, dismemberment and resurrection were the enactment of an essential mystery. As the body of Osiris was first drowned, so the Nile flooded the land to make it fertile. As his corpse was then broken and scattered, so the seeds of the grain crops had to be scattered in the ground. As Isis called him forth to life, so the earth harbored and nourished the kernels until they sprouted and rose up golden in the sight of the sun.

Yet, as the resurrected Osiris reminded his Queen, the grain must be threshed and winnowed and the corn sent down into the earth once again to bring forth the next year's harvest. Therefore he, though brought back to life, chose to go down to the underworld and rule there among the dead. He would be their patron and protector, and would serve as a beacon to mark the path that all departed souls had to follow. Forever after, all voyagers into the world beyond would adopt the name of Osiris in the funeral rites that accompanied their passing. They would be provided with maps and guides to help them find their way through the labyrinthine land of the dead, and would follow in the footsteps of Osiris on that dark journey.

Isis let her husband go. She knew that he, unlike a mortal, could move between the worlds at will; they would not be separated for long. For, in one respect, Osiris was like any earthly father: He wished to oversee the upbringing and education of his son, and would return to the land of the living to take a hand in it. He came frequently from his hidden home to tutor the boy in the disciplines of peace and war, of piety and kingship. He found his son an apt and willing pupil, preternaturally solemn and aware of the heavy obligations he was born to.

Isis used all her sorcery and all her wits to shelter the young god Horus from harm as he grew. He may just have been unlucky, or he may have been the target of his uncle Set's malevolence, but his childhood was marked by an inordinate number of accidents and misfortunes: Wild animals savaged the boy, scorpions plunged their pincers into his tender flesh, cramps and colics attacked his entrails. The spells his mother employed to

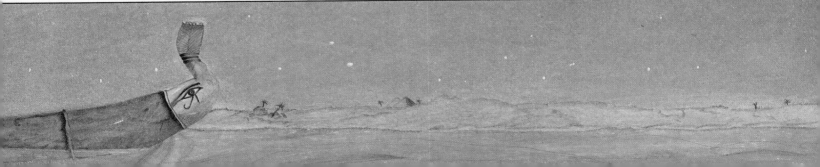

heal him became the foundations of curative magic and medicine. When she was not fending off these perils, Isis instructed him in wisdom, while Osiris returned from his abode in the kingdom of the dead to assess the youth's progress in the arts of war. Thus prepared to defend his royal line, Horus rose to manhood.

Set bided his time. It may have been that he was waiting for the stripling to grow into an opponent worthy of a fight. But Set dallied too long, and his nephew struck the first blow. To avenge the murder of his father, Horus gathered together a vast army of followers and launched a war against Set.

Caught unprepared, Set's troops fled the barrages of arrows, spears and lances wielded with deadly accuracy by Horus and his troops. Being themselves minor gods, or—as some tellers would have it—demons, the soldiers of Set were quick to resort to magic means when their military tactics failed. They transformed themselves into crocodiles, hippopotamuses and antelope. Armor turned to hide and horn, teeth to tusks, swords and spears to lashing tails. But this stratagem proved worse than useless. The battalions of Horus harried them into the wilderness, discovered their hiding holes and hacked the beasts to pieces.

Set, as the deity of war and violence, was not so easily subdued. He summoned up more soldiers and launched fresh attacks. For every defeat he suffered, he inflicted one on Horus. One battle spawned another, and the balance of power volleyed back and forth between the two. Uncle and nephew were of the same divine breed and shared in equal measure the cunning and bravado of their royal house. But the time came when the other deities grew weary of these never-ending wars.

The family of gods assembled in council and resolved that the power struggle should be ended by arbitration. They appointed the god Thoth, lord of the moon, to be judge of the tribunal.

All-perfect in wisdom, Thoth had served as a vizier and trusted counselor to the lord Osiris during the years when he and Isis ruled the earth together. He had earned the respect of gods and the awe of mortals, who agreed that Thoth alone could persuade the contenders to lay aside their arms.

None could fault him as the perfect choice. Thoth was eloquent—indeed, some chroniclers claimed he had invented speech—and levelheaded. For he was the measurer of time and the father of mathematics, who helped gods and mortals keep a count of their wealth and their obligations. To him belonged the allegiance of those whose skills depended on common sense, clear vision and scrupulous attention to detail: astronomers, canal-builders, treasurers and accountants, architects of pyramids and palaces.

On the day appointed for the trial's beginning, the great river was crowded with the barques of the gods. No member of the pantheon would absent themselves from so momentous an event. White sails billowed with the wind from the north, speeding the vessels of those deities who dwelled downstream and traveled upward against the current. From the opposite direction came ships rowed by slaves, plying their oars in rhythm to the helmsman's chanted orders.

The barques waited at the landing place, allowing the deities to disembark in unhurried decorum. As each god and goddess stepped onto the shore, sparkling with gold and radiant in pleated robes of creamy linen, the watching populace on shore and the watermen in their feluccas were all transfixed by the sight.

When Set arrived, looking neither to right nor left, the crowd began to murmur; when Horus landed, accompanied by his mother Isis, the hum grew to a roar. From the highest lords of creation to the lowliest laborers carrying their baskets along the river's muddy banks, all Egypt knew that the outcome of this trial would decide their fortunes. They waited in hope and terror.

None but the gods themselves were permitted to enter the lofty chamber designated for the trial. Magisterial in manner, Thoth presided over a court as solemn as that underworld tribunal where Osiris now sat in judgment over the souls of the newly dead. But, whereas Osiris and his jackal-headed lieutenant, Anubis, weighed the heart of each defendant in the scales of justice, it would be Thoth's lot to weigh the rival claims to kingship.

Many divine witnesses were called to offer testimony. Some statements favored Set's claim to the throne; others were on the side of Horus. And all the participants acquitted themselves with such eloquence and sincerity that the listeners found themselves swayed constantly from one view to the opposite, quite unable to make up their minds.

When Set's champions held forth, the audience found itself incensed at the injustices he had suffered and the grievances he had nursed since the very first days of his brother Osiris' earthly reign. When those who pressed the claims of Horus took the floor, the company was moved to tears at all that Isis' young son had been forced to suffer at the hands of a wicked uncle who wished him nothing but ill.

A great many long-established laws and age-old precedents were called upon and challenged, concerning property rights, territorial agreements, and the necessary attributes of one who would rule the world. Set insisted that he, as lord of war and slayer of monstrous serpents, should gain the throne in recognition of his superior strength; by virtue of his age he was far more fit than his stripling nephew to wear the crown. Horus, in his turn, spoke of rights of primogeniture and direct lineage, invoking the ideal of divine justice to turn his hearers' hearts.

It was said by some chroniclers that the trial continued for as long as eighty years, until it reached an impasse. Then the moon-god took it upon himself to bring matters to a conclusion.

He had listened without comment to Horus' declaration of his right, as son of Osiris, to assume the throne. He had said nothing when Set rose up and disputed his nephew's paternity. But when the god of war asked why anyone should believe the farfetched tale concocted by the witch

Horus, son of Isis and Osiris, warred against his uncle Set for the
throne. In the heat of the bitterest battle, Set's routed followers took
the shapes of crocodiles, hippopotamuses and other wild creatures.

Judged by Thoth to be the rightful ruler, Horus presided over Egypt's growing

greatness, and fathered the royal house that would lead it through a millenium of glory.

Isis to account for the conception of her bastard whelp, Thoth knew that the time for decision had come.

The silence lay heavy on the court as Thoth pondered. Finally, he announced that the young god Horus, son of Osiris in the line of Ra, was the sole legitimate ruler of the kingdom of Egypt.

The chroniclers were silent on Set's reaction to this judgment, but he did not contest it, nor try to counter it. It was written on the walls of certain pyramids that he was banished to the desert. But some storytellers claimed that he turned into a black pig, and swallowed up the moon each month when it vanished from the sky, seeking to take vengeance on Thoth, the lunar god, for deciding in his enemy's favor. From that day forward, Horus governed in peace, as did his descendants after him who wore the double crown of Egypt as Pharaohs and living gods. They would be worshipped as divinities by their subjects, feared, adored and cloaked in mystery.

For ending the turmoil of generations, Thoth was honored with the title "He who judges the two companions." And it was said by the ancient sages that without Thoth, the long and intricate tale of the sun-god, Ra, and his divine descendants would never have been told. For, as well as making peace between the deities, Thoth brought their subjects one other blessing. He taught them the potent magic of forming words from pictures, so that all future ages might learn for themselves the truth of what had happened.

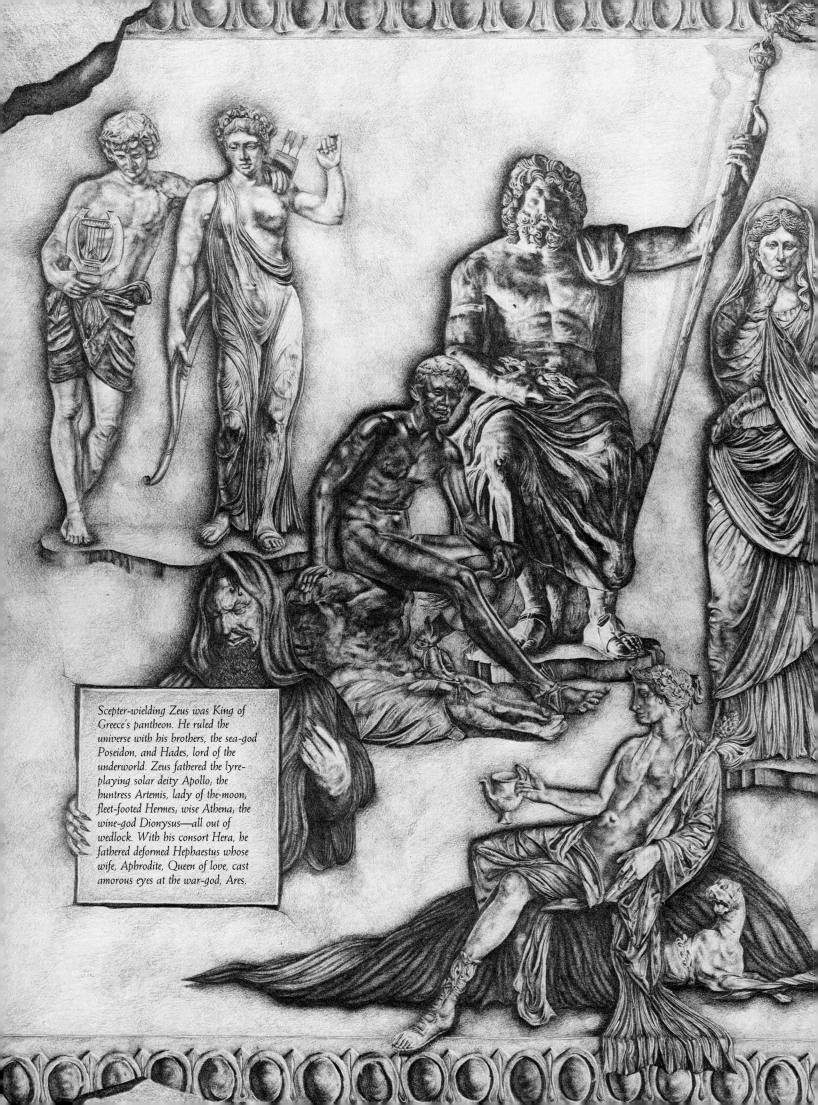

Scepter-wielding Zeus was King of
Greece's pantheon. He ruled the
universe with his brothers, the sea-god
Poseidon, and Hades, lord of the
underworld. Zeus fathered the lyre-
playing solar deity Apollo, the
huntress Artemis, lady of the-moon,
fleet-footed Hermes, wise Athena, the
wine-god Dionysus—all out of
wedlock. With his consort Hera, he
fathered deformed Hephaestus whose
wife, Aphrodite, Queen of love, cast
amorous eyes at the war-god, Ares.

Two

The Passions of Olympus

Beneath the cerulean skies of ancient Greece, a proud race of dreamers sang the chronicles of their gods. The land these poets dwelled in was no paradise of peace and plenty. For many centuries, empire-building tyrants menaced its scattered settlements. Men slept with their spears by their sides; women rose early to goad the sullen earth with hoes of bone and plows of iron, struggling to eke out a living from parched and stony soil.

Yet in one resource their homeland was rich beyond all measure: the genius of its inhabitants. From their scrutiny of nature's mysteries, philosophy was born. The statues they raised for worship and remembrance idealized the human form and glorified the human spirit. And in their magnificent stone amphitheaters they praised their gods in ritual dance and measured choruses that echoed across time. Their deities controlled all the great rhythms and hazards of the universe: moonrise, sunset, tide, rain, the lambing of ewes and the haul of fish in the mariner's net.

Born when the blood of a dying deity mingled with foam from the sea, Aphrodite was the goddess of love and beauty. Her provocative gaze concealed her terrible power of blighting or blessing human lives.

All things emanated from the will of the immortals. If the sea raged and a ship foundered, Poseidon, ruler of the waters, had commanded it because he was displeased with the sailors; if strangers were entranced and enamored at first meeting, it was because Aphrodite, Queen of love, had touched them in the root of their being; if a woman died in labor, it was because the goddess of childbirth had been detained elsewhere.

The world was dangerous, yet available to a certain kind of manipulation. It was well known that a safe voyage could be guaranteed, or a healthy birth assured, by precautionary rituals of sacrifice and worship to honor or cajole the heavenly powers. The deities were eminently susceptible to such attentions, for they were themselves men and women, with features and characters as clearly defined as any mortal hero's. Through their ranks rode the full cavalcade of human virtues, vices, ambitions and desires.

The Greek poets who recorded the history of the gods drew from an inexhaustible treasury of myth and memory. Every island in their archipelago was the site of some heroic struggle or celestial lovers' tryst. The tales of the deepest past recounted a time of blood and battle, when Zeus and his siblings strove to wrest control of the universe from an older generation of deities. And once the rule of Zeus on Olympus was assured, the lore was further enriched by stories of his amorous encounters and quarrels, and by the wonders performed by his kin.

Their family tree was intricate, indeed incestuous. The children of Zeus, both lawful and illegitimate, swelled the pantheon. Some were conceived before Zeus assumed the Olympian throne, others were born when his hegemony was secure. On the fine points of their chronology, the storytellers were imprecise and often contradictory.

It was plain to every Greek that all the gods were fallible. At root, their authority was undermined by the savage history of their rise to power. The story of the celestial revolution had its beginning in a place where time itself had not even been born. Here, brooding in the void of infinite darkness, was Chaos.

How Chaos had sprung into being mortals could never fathom; but it was known that out of Chaos came Gaea—Earth—the warm, fertile mother of creation. From Gaea was born Uranus, the vast canopy of the sky, crowned with stars. Gaea's equal in majesty, Uranus became not only son but husband. Their union bore many children: first, the Titans, six male and six female giants, the first mortal race to people the universe; next, the Cyclopes, as mighty in bearing as their siblings, but each with only one eye glaring from the center of his forehead; finally, the Hecatoncheires, three grotesquely deformed monsters, each one with a hundred arms and fifty heads.

Uranus witnessed the births of each of his progeny with increasing horror. He became possessed by the conviction that these brutish children would one day rise up and murder him. Even as they struggled—fully grown—

from Gaea's womb, he grabbed them and flung them into a deep, jagged pit where he left them to die. Gaea wailed her sorrow to the skies. Monsters they may have been, but her maternal feelings extended even to the most grotesque.

Her misery festered into desire for revenge. Drawing from the secret reaches of her heart a river of bright, boiling metal, Gaea forged a sickle that was strong enough to raze a mountain. She descended to the pit where her children languished and showed them the weapon. She asked which one of them would dare to wield the blade against their evil parent. Of all their number, only Cronus, a Titan, raised his hand.

That night, as Uranus lay sprawled beside Gaea, deep in sleep, Cronus—smuggled from the chasm and lying hidden in the copious folds of his mother's body—crept out. He snatched up the sickle and, with one stroke, hacked off the sky-god's genitals and flung them into the sea. As Uranus screamed, a torrent of black blood erupted from his wound. Where it fell, the ground split open and threw up a horde of giants, and at their side the Furies—evermore to be the persecutors of offending mortals.

The severed pieces of Uranus' body, floating in a bloody spume at the ocean's edge, burst into a brilliant foam. A female figure appeared riding the crest of the breaker as it cascaded to the shore. In this way did Aphrodite, the goddess of love, come into the world.

With Uranus crippled and useless, the universe lay at Cronus' feet. At once he returned to the chasm and set free his brothers and sisters, the Titans. The Cyclopes and Hecatoncheires he unwisely left behind in the dark. Now Cronus, the usurper, continued the task of creation. He took as his bride his sister Rhea, and together they produced two sons, Hades and Poseidon, and three daughters, Demeter, Hera and Hestia.

But the wheel of fortune ground its inexorable course: Cronus looked at his children and was afraid. Why should they not do what he had done to his father, Uranus? In a torment of fear and anger, Cronus tore Hades and Poseidon away from their mother's breast and swallowed them alive.

Rhea gave birth to her next child in a secret place, then returned home and docilely offered Cronus something swaddled in a blanket. Without hesitation, Cronus snatched the bundle and swallowed it. But this time the devious Cronus was himself fatally deceived. A smooth stone now lay in Cronus' belly, while Zeus, the son of Rhea, was saved. The infant god was handed by his grandmother Gaea into the care of the Curetes, high priests of Crete. He grew to maturity unmolested.

One afternoon a hooded sibyl came to Cronus, offering auguries. The warning froze his blood: He was destined to be murdered by one of his own sons. Yet all of them, he knew, had been devoured. Scowling, he summoned his handmaiden, the reticent young goddess Metis, to bring him a soothing drink. And in so doing, he gave a helping hand to fate. For Zeus, now grown to manhood, was Metis' paramour, and with his collusion the drink had been drugged.

Cronus began vomiting, and from his gorge hurtled all those he had swallowed up—Demeter, Hera and Hestia, Hades and Poseidon—wretched and bewildered but unharmed by their ordeal. Weak with nausea and fear, Cronus was no match for Zeus and his siblings. The broken Titan was hauled out of the sky and riveted to a boulder beneath the sea bed, doomed to weep away eternity.

Zeus immediately began to consolidate his position before the Titans could rally and attack him. Choosing Mount Olympus for the center of his command, he drew about him a company of immortals to defend the craggy stronghold.

The onslaught, when it came, was cataclysmic. For ten years the Titans bombarded Olympus without a second's respite; for ten years the rebels held their ground. At last, seeing no end to this war of attrition, Zeus plunged into Tartarus, the grisliest dungeon of Hell, and freed the Cyclopes and Hecatoncheires. Prisoners first of Uranus, then Cronus, then long forgotten, they owed allegiance to Zeus, their deliverer, and not to their brothers the Titans.

With the Hecatoncheires and the Cyclopes behind him, Zeus was equipped to devastate his enemies. Standing astride the peak of Mount Olympus, the son of Rhea hurled thunderbolt after thunderbolt, until the rocks beneath the Titans' feet boiled to a bubbling paste and the sea itself was aflame. Only then did they surrender. Zeus, exhausted, bound the Titans with massive chains, dragged them down into the very bowels of the earth and entombed them there.

But the trials of Zeus were not finished yet. Another chronicle told how Gaea, who had once been his benefactress and savior, had grown weary of the havoc spawned by Zeus's ambition. In one surge of desperate creation, she wrenched out of herself the monster Typhon and set him to attack Olympus.

Typhon was an awesomely powerful beast and vile to behold. His eyes rolled like a rabid dog's and bled fire; his thighs were a writhing mass of vipers; his hands and stinking black tongue convulsed and flailed continually; he was so tall his head scraped against the sky. At the sight of him, the gods—not injudiciously—ran all the way to Egypt. All except Zeus, who locked with Typhon in close combat. But the contest was unequal. Entangled in the slithering net of snakes, Zeus fell, and Typhon slit open the young god's body with his talons. Rescued by his son Hermes while the creature gloated, Zeus tied his own wounds and immediately returned to the fight—armed this time with thunderbolts.

The monster was caught off guard. Dazzled by the lightning flashes and scorched by the blasts, Typhon bellowed in despair and staggered away to Sicily, where Zeus buried him under Mount Etna. There the creature remained trapped, writhing in agony and blasting flames of hate at Heaven.

Now Zeus was truly master of the universe. Calling together the faithful

veterans of his campaign, he decreed that Olympus should remain their shared and permanent home. Here would they bask in the luxuries for which they had fought so bitterly and long. Let the sun rise from hiding to take its rightful place in the sky and let nectar pour like rain in celebration of their victory. The deities cheered, laughed, and burst into raucous song.

Zeus lifted his hand for silence. First, he said, there was a matter to be settled in the presence of all the gods. Resting his arms on the shoulders of his brothers Hades and Poseidon, he told the assembled immortals how the precedent of murdering one's family rivals had now to be broken: He intended to share his power, not to hoard it. The world would therefore be separated into three domains, and he would draw lots with his brothers for possession of them. So saying, he held out the anklebones of a sheep to spin as dice. One by one the brothers rolled the bones to find their kingdoms; and so it was that Hades came to rule the

After victory against the gods who preceded them, the brothers Zeus, Hades and Poseidon cast lots to determine the territory each would rule. Their dice were the anklebones of sheep; their prizes the mastery of air, sea and underworld.

underworld, Poseidon the sea, and Zeus the air and all that breathed it.

Undoubtedly, Zeus had won the greatest share—but this came as a surprise to no one. The ability to predict the behavior of sheep's bones was hardly beyond the powers of the god of supreme wisdom. Nevertheless, the gesture was a triumph of diplomacy, and Zeus's status as a just and wise leader was, for the present, firmly established. While the young gods had learned from the harsher fortunes of their ances-tors, and found it possible to live in the same place at the same time without plotting feverishly to murder one another, they sometimes fell to bickering over possessions, whether it was over lands or spouses. Usually such disputes were petty affairs, and it was possible to settle them diplomatically with the intervention of Zeus. But sometimes it was not; then humor and a readiness to listen to reason would collapse under such ignoble sentiments as avarice and pride.

One such conflict flared up between Poseidon and Athena, the bright-eyed daughter of Zeus. Her very presence on Olympus was a source of controversy. For all Zeus's rhetoric of sharing and conciliation, Athena was a living testament to a serious misdeed on his part.

As a young god on the verge of his ascent to the highest position among the immortals, Zeus had married Metis, the dissembling cup-bearer who had tricked Cronus. Just as his father had, Zeus became prey to the obsession that any children he engendered would grow up inclined to murder him in his bed. So when Metis brought her husband the news that she was pregnant, Zeus reverted to the habits of his forebears, swelled to a prodigious size and ate her.

Soon afterward, he began to suffer for his rashness. His head was racked with excruciating pains. At last, as he roared in agony, his forehead split open. Out sprang Athena, dressed in glittering armor and brandishing a javelin. From this moment on, Zeus doted hopelessly on this willful daughter to the exclusion and muted chagrin of the other gods. When Athena expressed a desire to become the patroness of Attica—a city-state of which Poseidon was particularly fond—the immortals feared the worst.

In those days, Attica was ruled by King Cecrops, an honorable and levelheaded man. When it was brought to Poseidon's attention that Athena unofficially numbered Attica among her personal effects, the sea-god ordered Cecrops to assemble his subjects as quickly as possible. His brother had elected to litter the universe with his privileged offspring: very well. But that privilege must not trespass on true divinity. He, Poseidon, lord of the oceans and ruler of the rivers, would show the citizens of Attica which god was worthy of their obeisance.

The tale-tellers diverged in their accounts of what Poseidon actually showed the bemused crowd. Some said he struck the acropolis with his trident and a salt-water spring leaped out of the solid rock; others claimed the thing that emerged was a horse—a creature unknown at that time in the mortal world. Whatever Poseidon's gambit, whether gift or demonstration of arcane power, it was not enough. Athena, waiting her turn, drew her hand gracefully into the air—and in its wake rose up an olive tree. The sheer elegance of this act of creation hushed the crowd into awed silence.

Poseidon was scandalized. Storming away to Olympus, he challenged his fellow immortals to voice their opinions. They had witnessed the entire episode, so whom did they consider the Atticans favored: her or him? This question put the gods in a quandary. It was dangerous to displease Poseidon; by the same token, the prospect of snubbing Zeus's daughter was equally unattractive.

After a great deal of shrugging and prevarication, the gods abdicated all responsibility by summoning Cecrops to give his opinion. The old King answered truthfully: Athena. At this, Poseidon flew into a rage and swamped Attica with a torrential flood. The city, however, recovered under Athena's care, and entered into new life as Athens—the capital city of the mortal world.

Another account related how Poseidon and Athena eventually resolved their differences by colluding as conspirators in an altogether more sinister dispute, culminating in mutiny against Zeus himself—a mutiny led by his wife Hera. For Zeus, infidelity to Hera was a favorite game, occupying a large proportion of his time, energy and imagination.

The subterfuges he used in his attempts to hide these escapades from his spouse were inventive but rarely successful. Inevitably, Hera became angry with his behavior. One morning, after a particularly strenuous night's philandering, the father of the gods returned to the marital home, made his excuses and retired to bed in pursuit of lost sleep.

White with anger, Hera vowed that Zeus would not defile their marriage again. She went out onto the sun-baked terraces of Olympus, where Athena and Poseidon lounged, bored and lethargic. Dashing cups of nectar from their hands, she harangued them: How long were they prepared to let that lecher, Zeus, continue to rule their lives with his boorish and whimsical commands? Had they no pride? Now was the time to put an end to his depraved tyranny—now, while he mumbled in his guilty sleep!

The gods were astonished. But Hera did not relent. Exciting the immortals' bloodlust with her tirade, she led the way to Zeus's bed. There the would-be assassins paused for a moment, uncertain of what to do. Then, at Hera's instigation, they bound the sleeper with a multitude of ropes to keep him prisoner while they meditated their next move.

Busy with their trussing, they did not notice the movement behind a curtain as Thetis, Zeus's current mistress, slipped away to raise the alarm. She summoned Briareus, largest of the hundred-handed Hecatoncheires and Zeus's faithful servant. With his help, Thetis soon freed her lover, who awoke to find himself surrounded by mountainous coils of untied rope, with Briareus feverishly unpicking the remaining knots.

When Zeus learned what had happened, he was furious with Hera. He dealt his wife the first of many severe beatings—as much for airing the problems of their marriage in public as for conspiring to kill him.

But Hera's will was not broken. The poets passed down an account of her machinations against one particularly hated rival. When she learned that the goddess Leto had conceived a child by Zeus, she determined to do everything in her considerable power to prevent either mother or child surviving the pregnancy.

To this end, Hera hounded Leto mercilessly as the wretched goddess wandered across the earth, searching vainly for a place to labor and give birth. Not a single mortal community, from the noblest city to the humblest hamlet, would allow Leto into its midst. Every time she came upon a new dwelling and

Sleeping Zeus was trussed for slaughter by his jealous wife, but hundred-handed
Briareus succored him, swiftly disentangling the knots that bound him.

Furious at her husband's infidelities, Hera summoned the serpent-dragon Python to hunt down Leto—one of Zeus's paramours—to the ends of the earth and devour her along with her illegitimate offspring.

knocked feebly at its door, the occupants would draw their bolts against her and hiss through knotholes that she should go away and take her curse elsewhere. For wherever Leto went, Hera had been there the day before, threatening to heap the most appalling retribution on anyone who dared to show the hapless goddess even the smallest charity.

Hera's commitment to this persecution campaign was total. She made a vow that if Leto was to be allowed to give birth at all, it would be in a place where the sun's rays could never penetrate. Eventually, Leto found herself marooned on a remote island in the middle of the Aegean sea, where Poseidon took pity on her. So that Hera's oath should not be violated, he drew the sea in a vast, sparkling cupola high over the island, shutting out the sun. Here, Leto finally bore her illegitimate twin babies, Apollo and Artemis.

Her labor had been long and agonizing, lasting nine days and nine nights. Hera had prevented Ilithyia, the goddess of midwifery, from coming until it was almost too late for the safety of both mother and babes. Some storytellers said that Artemis, the firstborn child, stood up and assisted her mother in the delivery of her brother Apollo, thereafter becoming the true patroness of childbearing, to whom all mothers would cry out in their pains.

Yet even while Leto rested after the exertions of her double labor, her enemy Hera was preparing a new horror to torment her rival: Hera loosed Python, and was guiding it to find and mangle Leto.

Python was a female snake-dragon that Gaea had fashioned long before in the war of the giants, to relieve her of the task of suckling her more hideous and violent offspring. Created to know itself only as a slave and killing machine, Python eagerly slithered after Hera, hungry to deal death and misery.

When the monster reached the island, it raised itself up to its full, horrifying height and plunged through the shield of seawater that was protecting Leto and her newborn babies. Poseidon, however, had no intention of allowing Python to disrupt his charge's peace. With his trident he churned the waters of the dome, and the monster was flung away, a flailing jungle of coils. In the fever of her labor, Leto had made a promise: that if—after all these torments—she could only be favored with a successful birth, she would entreat her son one day to consecrate the island by erecting upon it the finest, most beautiful temple the world had ever seen. When her travail was over, she took the twins with her to the land of her kinsfolk. It was not long before Apollo set out to honor his mother's pledge. At an age when most children could only mewl helplessly in their cradles, he stood tall and strong. Dressed in the finest armor and equipped with the sharpest arrows, the infant god journeyed as far as the vale of Crissa before he lay down in the lee of a hill to rest.

When he awoke, night had settled like a blanket on the quiet countryside around him. Sitting up under the stars, Apollo realized that he was completely lost; he had not the slightest idea where he was, or what direction he should take. Climbing to the brow of the hill upon which he had slept, the young warrior rested his hands on his hips and gazed despairingly out over the darkened meadows.

Then he saw a young woman standing a little way along the ridge. He did not know, said the chroniclers, that this was Telphousa, the nymph who ruled the valley. She had seen Apollo enter her territory and had been stalking him ever since like a predator, making herself invisible among the trees and in the hedgerows. She did not know who the stranger was, nor why he had come, but she could smell power on him—and she feared for her little kingdom.

Telphousa approached the young god and asked him what place it was he sought. At his reply, she smiled to herself and pointed to a range of mountains dimly visible in the moonlight. His path lay there, the nymph explained—through the narrow gorge of Parnassus. Apollo thanked his guide and immediately strode off down the hillside—little knowing that he had been betrayed. For the rocky path that wound through the gorge of Parnassus, as the nymph well knew, led to one destination only: Python. Deep in the wasteland, the beast had made its lair and was lying in wait, day after day, for living things to kill.

Apollo entered the deadly pass at dawn. No sooner had he stepped between the jagged walls than Python struck out. Wreathing its body around the god, the evil creature began to crush him with a strength that would have pulped a mountain. But Apollo wriggled free. Drawing his bow, he shot one arrow straight through Python's throat. With a howl of pain, the monster disgorged blood, thrashed violently, and died.

When Apollo returned to his mother after the successful completion of his mission, Leto braved the malevolence of Hera and showed Zeus the handsome twins. Their father gathered them up and cradled them on his knee. The baby girl, Artemis, shrieked with laughter and tugged at her father's beard. He was delighted with this engaging child and asked her what toys he could make to amuse her. All was in his gift.

Zeus was amazed when the baby sat up, regarded him levelly and declaimed a list of requests. She wanted the forests, mountains and all the wild places of the earth to rule as her domain; she desired a retinue of nymphs to attend to her every wish, and a hunting bow wrought of the finest silver.

After a short silence, Zeus asked if there was anything else his daughter might require? Yes, answered Artemis: She desired the gift of perpetual virginity.

At this, Zeus threw back his head, roared with laughter, and granted his daughter every one of her wishes. This last, he chuckled to Leto, who was hovering at his side in agitation, was indeed a strange request for a child of Zeus.

As Leto's twins grew up, they both assumed a multitude of sacred duties and responsibilities. Artemis became the goddess of the moon in all its changes, while Apollo ruled the sun and protected the many herds and flocks on earth. He was guardian also of a certain herd of holy cattle dedicated to his father Zeus, and in this role he became the victim of another of Zeus's love children—Hermes.

It was said by the storytellers that Hermes was still a babe in arms when he played this prank on Apollo. Left unattended in his cradle, supposedly asleep, Hermes slipped out of his nursery and ran to the land of Arcadia. On a hillside he found Apollo's heifers grazing across a lush pasture. Rounding up the fifty finest animals, Hermes quietly enticed them away and led them to a cave on the banks of the River Alpheus.

Apollo heard not a sound. Moreover, when he counted his beasts that evening and learned of the theft, he thundered off in the wrong direction to look for them: The wily Hermes had persuaded the cattle to walk backward, leaving a trail that led away away from their destination, not toward it.

Hermes, meanwhile, had banqueted privately and at leisure on the meat of several of his spoils. Carving the finest carcasses into twelve portions, he burned eleven of them in honor of the gods and ate the twelfth. This, said the sages much later, was the first recorded burned offering. Then, leaving the remainder of the heifers still tethered in the cave, the infant god crept home to his cradle to sleep off the feast.

By divine interrogation of bovine and other witnesses, Apollo soon learned who the culprit was and sought him out. Hermes feigned innocence. But Apollo well understood the vein of precocity in his family. Grabbing the child, he took him to stand trial before Zeus.

To Apollo's horror, though the facts of the robbery were soon established, Zeus appeared to find the whole episode amusing. He managed to hide his smiles, however, and commanded the little god to give the surviving cows back at once. Hermes instantly obeyed, thus endearing himself further to his sentimental father. Apollo, disgusted with all concerned, returned to Arcadia to sulk.

But Hermes made amends for his mischief with a gift that not only delighted Apollo but brought a new source of beauty to the world. Walking beside a stream on Olympus, Hermes found an empty tortoise shell. Inspired, he affixed strings to it, plucked them and produced sweet music that entranced all living things. Apollo, hearing its sound on the wind in Arcadia, hurried to Olympus to locate its source. Finding Hermes with his hand poised above the strings, he grimaced and turned to go; but Hermes called his name and, with a shy smile, offered him the lyre. Unable to resist

Young Hermes found a tortoise shell and used it to devise the world's
first lyre. Intrigued by the instrument's sweet sounds, Apollo befriended
Hermes, received the lyre as a gift, and became the patron god of music.

taking it, Apollo found that he himself had a marvelous aptitude for the instrument, and played and sang far into the night. Thus, through Hermes' peace offering, Apollo became the god of music.

Hermes and Apollo, like all but one of the children sired by Zeus, were paragons of physical perfection. Only Hephaestus was deformed from birth and grew up ugly. His feet were shapeless stumps of heavy flesh; his hips thrust out at a bizarre angle from his body; and his gait was painful and grotesque. His immortal kindred treated this alien in their midst with a contempt that barely masked their superstitious fear. Compassion was not among their virtues.

Hephaestus was the child of Zeus and Hera. It was widely rumored that he had been conceived out of wedlock during his parents' courtship, but this slander may well have been circulated purely in order to prick Hera's inflated sense of propriety. Whatever the circumstances of Hephaestus' birth, the boy was a constant source of embarrassment and shame to his proud mother.

Walking one day with her son, Hera found her progress attended by especially loud divine laughter. Hephaestus had disappeared from her side. Looking back, she saw him lying collapsed in a heap where he had tripped; he was quite unable to stand again without help, and stared at her with pathetic eyes.

Marching over to the frightened boy, Hera pulled him up by one of his legs and flung him over the parapet of Olympus.

The gods crowded to the edge to watch the child plummet into the sea below, then politely applauded Hera's uncompromising solution to her problem. Being immortal, Hephaestus survived the fall, and was taken into the care of Thetis, who dwelled under the sea.

There, despite his deformities, the boy grew broad and muscular—worthy at least in strength to be a champion of Olympus. Furthermore, closeted in his peaceful cavern under the waves, Hephaestus dedicated himself to all arts of design and manufacture: He learned how to forge exquisite shapes from wood, metal and the living rock around him. He delighted Thetis daily with gifts of ironwork and statuary; he designed fabulous machines to serve her and himself. As he hammered day and night at the colossal anvil he had invented, Hephaestus knew himself to be happy.

But happiness was not enough. After nine years' sojourn, Hephaestus found that a corner of his heart was irrevocably dedicated to repaying his mother some of the hurt she had done him. So the lame god's proficiency with his hands was turned to making a weapon to avenge the indignity of his expulsion from his former home on Olympus. He built a throne of the tawniest bronze, decorated it with delicate tracery and sent it anonymously to Hera as a gift. She was puzzled by its arrival but fascinated by its skillful artwork, and settled down in it to think.

Instantly, huge manacles sprang out of the arms of the throne, trapping Hera so tightly that she could not move even an inch. She cried out in terror, and the gods

Flung by his mother from the Olympian heights, Hephaestus plunged into the sea.

There, the sea nymph Thetis rescued him, and nurtured him until he grew to manhood.

rushed to find her, but even they could not free her from the grip of Hephaestus' shackles, for he alone understood the secret of their mechanism.

When the gods learned who was responsible for this humiliating trick, Ares was dispatched to drag Hephaestus from his hiding-place and beat him until he confessed how to work his machine. But the lad had grown to be a formidable opponent—a match even for the burly god of war. The immortals only succeeded in bringing the blacksmith out of his cave and back to Olympus by making him incapable with wine, a weapon that Hephaestus did not understand.

When he was sober enough to speak, however, the young god created still more confusion by shouting out that his price for Hera's release was the hand of Aphrodite. He would accept nothing less, and no torture imaginable could wring the secret from him. Hera would spend eternity strapped down.

At this declaration, a tremor of disgust ran through the assembled gods. The very idea of intimacy with the hideous Hephaestus was a profoundly unpleasant one. But Hera, surveying the immortals' frowning faces with mounting horror, allowed them not a moment longer to ponder the choice they must make. Let him take Aphrodite, she pronounced. The Queen of Heaven must be released.

So began the tale of one of the most extraordinary marriages ever to take place on Mount Olympus. The beast Hephaestus took the beauty Aphrodite for his bride, and suffered miserably for it ever after. Hephaestus adored Aphrodite and

tried everything to make her happy. But she tossed aside the toys and treasures he made for her, shrank from his embraces and began to take other lovers. She intimated quite directly to Ares, the war-god, that there might be a place for him in her bed when her husband was away. The god of war came running.

But Hephaestus was no fool. One day, he told his wife that a piece of work at his forge demanded very careful attention. It would, he regretted, require his absence from home for several days. Aphrodite looked dutifully distressed and waved her husband good-bye. Within the hour, she and Ares were cavorting on her marriage bed. Hephaestus, however, had gone no farther than the roof of his own house. The work that so urgently required his attention had in fact been finished days before and even now hung suspended from the bedroom ceiling. With a cry of triumph, Hephaestus cut the cords that sent a huge bronze net crashing down onto the bed, pinning the guilty couple together

A bride for the underworld

Once the world knew no winter and the flowers of all seasons bloomed together in glorious profusion. But then a mother's grief at the loss of her only daughter stamped a pattern on the year that would last forever. This is how it happened:

Persephone was the daughter of Demeter, Greek goddess of corn-fields and husbandry. One morning the girl wandered far from home through the lush green meadows of Sicily, gathering a scented bouquet to decorate her mother's house. Absorbed as she was in her search for the choicest blooms, Persephone heard neither the lark's song nor the hum of insects.

A sudden sharp crack, like the sound of a whip, broke the peace of the morning. Persephone saw a jagged gash open in the ground at her feet. From the widening fissure came an icy wind that scattered the flowers from her arms and blew her hair across her face. Four black horses thundered up out of the gloom, drawing a gleaming chariot. The driver, with reins held firmly in one hand, bent low over the frightened girl, encircled her waist with his free arm and snatched her up. Then, turning the horses, he drove full tilt back into the chasm. The earth closed up, and there was calm once again in the meadow.

At first Demeter may have found explanations for her daughter's prolonged absence: Perhaps she had forgotten the time as she chatted with nymphs, or had fallen asleep on the riverbank after bathing. Like any mortal mother in the same predicament, Demeter's mood swung

Persephone, gathering flowers, was abducted by Hades to the underworld.

violently. One moment the goddess fumed at the child's carelessness, the next she trembled, dreading a calamity. As dusk fell, Demeter knew that she would not sleep until she saw her daughter again.

She began a wearisome search through the world. Night and day she scoured groves and hills, riverbanks and seashores, calling until her voice grew harsh and her eyes dark-ringed with sorrow and fatigue.

Enraged by the ingratitude of once-loved lands that yielded no trace of Persephone, she cast blight upon them. Young shoots withered, ripening fruits rotted, mildew and mold attacked leaf and bud. The hungry people cried to Zeus for help as their food stores diminished, but they had no corn for an offering, no wine for a libation.

The desolate mother went again to Sicily and renewed her search in the old haunts. Finally, where the waters of an underground stream surfaced to fill a sheltered pool, she came upon a nymph who had heard the clatter of horses' hooves and the screams of a girl echoing through subterranean passages and caves. The nymph gave Demeter a ribbon Persephone must have let fall as she struggled with her captor. He was none other than Hades, god of the underworld.

Demeter sped to high Olympus. Wrathful that a fellow god had caused her such distress, she demanded that Zeus use his power to make Hades return the girl. She pointed to the barren lands and warned that nothing would grow until her daughter was set free.

Combing the world for her daughter, Demeter found only a scrap of her clothing.

49

Zeus knew that Hades had long harbored a passion for Persephone; he was unsurprised by news of her abduction by the god of the underworld. True to his own lascivious nature, Zeus had more sympathy for the lusts of a lover than for the grief of a mother, yet he could not allow famine to decimate humankind.

Finally he dispatched his messenger, Hermes, to the underworld with words of persuasion for Hades. He asked him to put aside his own desires for the greater good.

Hermes discovered the god of the underworld whispering sweet words into the ear of the silent Persephone. After the violence of the abduction, Hades had sought to gain her love by gentler means. So movingly did he speak of his deep, undying ardor that no maiden could fail to be thrilled. But still she was too distressed to eat or drink.

Hades received the message that Hermes bore with remarkable calm. He pondered for a moment, then suddenly was all compliance; he would take Persephone back to her mother himself. While the servants harnessed the horses, he began to eat a pomegranate. He offered a half to Persephone. With lowered eyes, she shook her head in refusal. He offered her a quarter. Again she shook her head, but more gently this time, and the merest hint of a smile hovered over her face. As if to catch that smile, the first she had given him since she came to his world, Hades lightly touched her mouth with his fingertips, and as if by accident pressed a pomegranate seed onto Persephone's lip.

At Demeter's behest, Hermes went as envoy to Hades to retrieve the maiden.

But now the horses were ready, and the couple mounted the chariot. As the steeds were whipped into movement, Persephone brushed her tongue across her lips, the seed was taken into her mouth and, unaware, she swallowed it.

The halls of Olympus reverberated with the sounds of Demeter's joy as she greeted her daughter. They clung to one another, kissing and exclaiming. But all that delight was turned again to devastating grief as Hades spoke in triumph of the swallowed seed. He reminded his fellow deities of an ancient and immutable law: Anyone who traveled between the upper and lower worlds was forbidden to partake of food or drink in the subterranean realms. Those who did so were bound to remain there forever.

Demeter bowed her head in acceptance of the rule that could never be changed. With Persephone lost, she resolved to leave Olympus. Orchards, fields and gardens would be eternally barren: Nothing would grow in the world again.

Zeus caught Demeter by the hand and stretched an arm around Hades' shoulder. There must, he said, be some compromise to avert such disaster. And so it was agreed. Persephone would stay with Demeter for two thirds of the year; during the remaining four months she would dwell with Hades in the underworld as his Queen.

Forever after, winter gripped the world while Demeter mourned Persephone's absence. But yearly the earth grew bright with the flowers of spring to welcome her return.

When Hades released Persephone for part of every year, Demeter rejoiced.

To catch his wife in the act of betrayal, Hephaestus set
a trap. From the ceiling above the violated marriage bed,
a net descended to imprison Aphrodite and her lover Ares.

in the most compromising of positions. Cackling maniacally, the cuckold scurried down from the rooftop and hobbled about Olympus, calling all the immortals to come and see the spectacle that he had arranged for them.

When they learned that the show consisted of ogling the tangled nudities of Ares and Aphrodite, the goddesses refused to attend; the gods, however, were less troubled by the prospect, and elbowed their way into the bedroom where they stood jostling for the best view.

This part of his plan worked against Hephaestus: The sight of Aphrodite inflamed such desire in both Hermes and Poseidon that each swore silently to take her as a lover himself. Subsequently, Aphrodite became the mistress of them both. Hephaestus trebled his own misery at a stroke, and earned the dangerous disapproval of Zeus, who had a vested interest in prohibiting the spread of such tactics among suspicious husbands.

Zeus's appetite for the female sex was insatiable. He would consider seriously any means of conquering his targets' affections or of taking them by surprise: He had appeared to his various mistresses as a bull, a swan, a cloud, once even as a shower of gold. Nor did he restrict his attentions to nymphs and goddesses alone. Having created mortal women to populate the earth, Zeus discovered that he had opened the door to a new world of potential conquests. But amorous liaisons with the fairest of his creations did not always turn out to be as uncomplicated or trouble-free as Zeus had hoped. This was a lesson cruelly taught him by Hera

Pregnant with Zeus's child, the mortal Princess Semele received a visit from an aged stranger. Unaware that the crone was Hera in disguise, Semele followed advice that led to her own destruction.

when she learned that her wayward husband had become infatuated with Semele, the daughter of King Cadmus.

The fact that the maiden was only a mortal did little to improve Hera's temper, and she immediately descended to the earth to seek out the young girl. Disguising herself as a wrinkled but kindly-looking crone, Hera introduced herself to Semele as a country nurse and asked if there was any way that she could be of service to the young Princess.

Semele, who after the great fertility-god's first visit had begun to suspect that she was pregnant, eagerly engaged Hera to attend her. Here, at last, was a sympathetic ear for all her troubles. The maidservants who had tended her from babyhood would be sure to tell her father if they found out that she had a secret lover. Hera brushed Semele's hair as the girl poured out her heart, clucking gently in amazement at every new description of this mysterious man.

Learning that he had promised Semele anything she asked for, the nurse made a suggestion. Why not insist that he reveal his true identity? A girl ought to know the father of her child, after all. Semele agreed that this was sensible, and she bade her confidante goodnight.

In the hours of thickest darkness, unseen by mortal or god, Zeus stole into Semele's bedchamber as he had done many times and lay down beside her. The Princess was wide awake and staring fixedly at the ceiling. Hera's friendly admonition had sowed a nagging anxiety in her mind: Who was this man who visited her in her bed night after night? She had never seen even the outline of his face. He could be a demon.

In a flurry of tearful confusion, Semele begged Zeus to tell her who he was, to show himself plainly for her to see and understand. Zeus's silence spoke his refusal, but Semele shrank from his caresses and insisted. He had promised her anything, and this was what she wanted. Was he a man of honor or not?

With a groan of despair, Zeus arose and threw off the mortal body he had assumed in order to smooth the path of his seduction of Semele. In that instant, night was blinded into brilliant day, the palace of Cadmus shaken to its foundations, and Semele scorched to a cinder by her lover's terrible beauty. Through his own boasting, Zeus had created the perfect trap for Hera to catch him in; in effect, he had appointed himself his mistress's executioner.

Sifting through Semele's charred remains, Zeus retrieved the immortal fetus she had carried. Then he performed an act of expiation. The mortal mother had died through his folly; now he would harbor the child within his own body and carry it to term. Slitting open his thigh, he placed the half-formed babe inside and diligently sewed up the wound.

Yet Hera was not satisfied with the extent of her revenge. She craved to annihilate every trace of Semele's relationship with Zeus. She needed to kill their child. Well acquainted with the murderous tenacity of Hera's jealousy, Zeus rightly feared for the baby nestling in his flesh.

Rescuing dead Semele's unborn child, Zeus sheltered it inside his
own thigh until it came to term. Thus Dionysus, the only god
with mortal blood, entered the world without a mother's labor.

When the skin of his swollen thigh had drawn so tight that it could only burst, Zeus cut free the infant and held him up to the light. He named the child Dionysus and secretly confided him to the care of Ino, Semele's sister, believing that Hera would not think to search for the boy in the mortal world.

But not only did Hera know exactly where to find Dionysus, she had already recruited the Titans from the vaults of the earth to help her slaughter him. With a wave of her arm, she scattered seeds of madness over the home of Ino's family. Malice sparkling in her eyes, Hera watched as the entire household plunged out into the street. The servants barked like dogs and bit at one another's throats in fury; Ino, foaming at the mouth and nose, tore out the heart of her own son and tried to eat it; little Dionysus, unattended, ran crying through the center of the carnage—straight into the clutches of the waiting Titans. Falling on the child, the giants ripped him apart with their hands and flung the bloody pieces into a boiling caldron.

Yet Dionysus survived. The goddess Rhea, the boy's grandmother, scoured out the residue caked onto the sides of the pot and clasped it to her breast. Exerting all her fantastic powers of fertility, Rhea throbbed life into the wreckage of Dionysus. Miraculously, her embrace resurrected the child, who was unscarred by his ordeal. Zeus now deliberated his son's future with greater care. On his instruction, Hermes, the master of disguises,

transformed Dionysus into a ram and smuggled him, unseen by Hera, to the foothills of Mount Nysa. Here, returned to his immortal self, the boy was tended day and night by nymphs, as Zeus himself had been. The maidens nourished him with milk and honey, and young Dionysus grew tall and proud—a true heir to the highest echelons of Olympus.

Hera, however, had other plans for the boy, and her persecution of him was faithfully recorded by the bards. Her spies were everywhere. She soon learned of her victim's extraordinary revival and escape, and the location of his hiding-place. Looking down on Mount Nysa from the dizzying heights of Olympus, Hera allowed herself a sour and lethal smile, certain that she would not fail again. The legacy of Semele's seduction would finally be purged. Hera mingled a curse with the raindrops that fell on the vine-covered slopes of Nysa. She willed Dionysus into a state of permanent drunkenness. By this means, she hoped, he would squander his life away in excess, and Zeus would disown him for shame.

But Hera was cheated of her vengeance once more. For Dionysus was blessed by the company of his elderly tutor, Silenus, an incorrigible rogue but the most loyal friend the young god could wish for. When the madness struck Nysa, he recognized at once the handiwork of Hera. Roaring drunk himself and scarcely able to walk, Silenus loaded the boy aboard a donkey and staggered off to seek the advice of the Oracle. There, the tutor and his pupil learned the nature of their affliction: The fermented juices of the grape

57

had the power to cheer, arouse, inspire, or even to drive a drinker mad. Armed with this knowledge, Dionysus and Silenus set out on an anarchic mission—to share with mankind the gift of wine.

But Hera's weapon was a powerful one. Neither god nor teacher could properly master the discipline of imbibing moderately; the pleasures of intoxication were too strong. After a time, their journey degenerated into an odyssey of brawling and lechery and murder. A wild army of satyrs—brutish creatures, half man and half goat—collected around the young god and contracted his madness. Everywhere Dionysus went, this ragged legion followed. Wherever he stopped, an orgy of savage revelry began. He was the crazed center of a dangerous carnival, always on the move.

Rhea, once before the savior of her ill-starred grandchild, followed Dionysus' rampage across the continents with increasing anxiety. Surely now—even at the risk of incurring Hera's anger—she should intervene and return the boy to his senses? Interrupting Dionysus' wanderings at Phrygia, Rhea took hold of the boy and, by rites and incantations, exorcised his madness. Now, she explained, the time had come for him to take up his rightful place among the noblest of the gods; but first he must voyage to the tranquil island of Naxos and there make himself fit for the destiny he had so long evaded. Dionysus surveyed his entourage of rioters and saw that this was a journey he must undertake alone.

Leaving his companions slumped in drunken exhaustion, the young god slipped away into the night and felt his way through the trees and down to the harbor. Rocking gently in the iron light of early dawn was a small craft; here and there he saw the silhouettes of crewmen at work on the docks and in the rigging. The ship was getting ready to sail. Clattering down the quayside, Dionysus called out to them: Were they sailing to Naxos? The sailors fell silent and peered at him curiously; he could not see their faces. Yes, one said, after a pause, and welcomed him aboard. Eagerly Dionysus scrambled onto the deck, burrowed into a pile of rags in the prow, and fell asleep.

When he awoke, the sun was high in a blue sky. Looking out over the waves, he could plainly see a sandy coastline stretching out along the horizon. He asked the sailors whether this was Naxos. No, they laughed, it was Egypt, where all the passengers,   including him, were

Inflamed by wine, Dionysus gathered a band of followers and ran riot through the world, spreading the gift and the curse of intoxication.

to be sold as slaves in the market. Never before had their regular cargo delivered itself aboard voluntarily. Dionysus solemnly urged them to reconsider and set a course for Naxos. The pirates guffawed and slapped their thighs.

Then Dionysus struck. In an instant, the decks became awash with sweet wine; vines erupted out of the mainmast and infested the sails, clawing them down in a tangled heap; wild beasts—the like of which the men had only met in nightmares—sprang out from the hatches and prowled the deck. Dionysus himself became a lion, cornering the crewmen who in their terror struck out at him with their oars. When the oars turned to snakes in their hands, the pirates hurled themselves overboard in despair. As they splashed into the water, Dionysus turned them to dolphins. Only the ship's pilot was spared this fate. Hoisting him on board, Dionysus asked if they might now continue to the appointed destination? Speechless with fright, the pilot tamed the frantic spinning of the ship's wheel and guided the vessel toward Naxos.

Through the performance of these and other wonders, he became known and feared throughout Greece as a great and powerful god—an ineluctable force in the lives of men and, especially, of women.

Wherever Dionysus paused, the women flocked in droves to join his orgiastic rites. Some said that here lay the true cause of Hera's obsessive persecution of her husband's love child: For by the sexual license that his cult bestowed upon female followers, Dionysus endangered the institution of marriage—of which Hera was the dedicated guardian.

The wild god raged on. He careered downward into the bowels of Hell, where he discovered his mother Semele huddled in the darkness. Using his divine powers, he restored her to the world of the living once again. But time finally cooled his frenzy. He ascended, at last, to claim his place on Olympus. There, the goddess Hestia, hard-pressed custodian of domestic harmony, willingly surrendered up to him her seat among the gods, so that the company of ruling divinities should remain at the sacred number of twelve.

With Dionysus enthroned, the assembly of Mount Olympus was complete. Now every aspect of the human temperament—from love to bellicosity, from lawfulness to anarchy—had its embodiment within the pantheon. The gods reigned not as faceless mysteries, but as the mirrors of humankind.

Kidnapped by pirates, Dionysus took a
terrible revenge, causing vines to ensnare the
vessel and wild beasts to roam its decks.

61

The Morrigan
Spectral Queen of War and its Wake

The Morrigan, High Queen and goddess of the Tuatha Dé Danann, watched over the welfare and warfare of that fairy folk while they struggled against the Firbolg people to claim the soil of Ireland. But the bards and blind harpers, who lulled warriors to rest at night after days of grueling battle, conveyed this paradox: The Morrigan was not one goddess, but a trinity. She was a single spirit of fierce intent, possessing at least three different names and a trio of separate selves.

Macha, they called her, when she worked magic with the blood of the slain. Badb, they named her, when she took a giantess's form and warned soldiers of their fortunes on the eve of war. And they knew her also as shape-shifting Neman. All three were wont to slide into the flapping black bodies of carrion crows to haunt battlefields, hungry for the morsels they filched from torn and broken bodies when the fray was done.

Terrible though they were, and feared as greatly by the Tuatha Dé Danann themselves as by their foes, the triad strove with all its superhuman strength to tip the war-scales in the Tuatha's favor. The singers in the halls of the mighty loved to recall the day when the Morrigan worked the Firbolg's undoing with firestorms, a hail of frogs, and torrents of blood that turned the ground into a steaming, sucking bog. By thus confounding the advancing enemy, the triple goddess bought time for her favored side, allowing the Tuatha to marshal their forces, hone their weapons sharp and bright, and win not only the war but Ireland itself.

Reaper of the battlefield

After a battle, Macha, the goddess of war, cloaked in the feathers of a carrion bird, looked on as the bodies of the slain were heaped up before her. Those of her chosen side were interred, with all due obsequies, under the great stones of their clans. But the foemen who had fallen were dismembered. Their freshly severed heads—some with battle cries still frozen on their lips, others with mouths fixed in the rictus of a fearful grin—were impaled on stakes and raised up in a ring to do her honor.

No tribute pleased her better. A warning to all her enemies, these henges, which were known as the masts of Macha, stood in the open countryside for all to see, while the birds and the elements worked their own transformations upon them.

Portender of calamity

When the morning mist still floated low over hill and moorland, a woman of giant dimensions came striding down to the river. Her legs, great columns of flesh, straddled the stream, and her feet rested on the stepping-stones of the ford as she bent to do her washing.

The clothes she scrubbed were not her own. In her great hams of hands they seemed as tiny as the swaddlings of a doll or an infant, yet they were the garments of full-grown soldiers bound for battle. And she, suffice to say, was no ordinary peasant laundress, but the goddess Badb, an aspect of the Morrigan.

Warriors on the march dreaded meeting Badb when they crossed a stream. For if they saw her wringing out clothes they recognized as their own, and the water ran red with blood, they knew they would not survive the clash to come.

Mother of mourning

She who loved war had also to love death, to celebrate it in a howling ecstasy of grief and lamentation. Some chroniclers maintained that, among the Morrigan's three incarnations, it was the elusive and enigmatic Neman who first devised the art of keening.

This ritual wailing was the music that accompanied the spirits of the dead to their final home. Torn first from the throats of newly made widows, the singing of these songs of loss became the prerogative of a sorority of black-clad crones. When the wagonloads of corpses trundled back from the fields of battle, the mourners' ululations filled the sky and drowned out the winds howling in from the sea.

It was said that whenever carrion birds screamed to one another over the bodies of the fallen, the voice of the Morrigan was heard in the land.

Three

Denizens of Eternity

Of all the old world's sages, none looked as deep into the distant past as the poets and mystics of India. They lived in a land that was encrusted with antiquity, steeped in time.

In the dusty air of the great central plain, the years hung as heavy as heat. To the south, along the great Coromandel Coast, the bones of a million generations of animals, the shells of snails and the scales of sea creatures were ground into sand by the ceaseless beating of the waves upon the shore. And far to the north, wind and water patiently reshaped whole mountain ranges, particle by infinitesimal particle.

The sages of that land perceived time as horizonless. It was a snake with its tail in its mouth, an endless cycle of creation and destruction that saw the passing of many universes, each possessing its own heaven and earth. With every new creation, human souls were born into joy or misery, as determined by their conduct in previous incarnations.

But the gods, perfect and immortal, reappeared entirely unchanged in each successive universe to manipulate nature. These divinities bore little resemblance to those of the West. The Olympian immortals, according to their chroniclers, were larger than life but still recognizably human. Their wars, passions and family quarrels were played out on a cosmic scale, but they looked like men and women and shared their weaknesses. The Indian deities, in contrast, were alien, otherworldly creatures. In hidden caves and sacred temples, the gods' carved and painted images inspired awe: Some had a multiplicity of arms, others the heads of elephants or simians; many were fleshed in brilliant rainbow hues, displayed by no known race on earth.

These gods, like all divinities, had the power to shift shape and to assume different identities at will. In some eras, they took new names and bodies without ever sacrificing the essential, ineffable qualities that made them who they were. Their wisdom was profound, their wits quicksilver, yet they were not devoid of human emotions—love and fear, hate and sorrow, jealousy and joy. Their deeds inspired a vast compendium of poetry and legends, and the sages in every epoch added their own accounts of fresh wonders to the lore: love stories, accounts of epic

battles between gods and demons, sagas of birth, death and rebirth.

The narrators were rarely precise as to chronology. The events they related took place in an unspecified but distant dreamtime that might have been the dawning of our own epoch or the final twilight of another.

The heavenly realm, sprawling across the snowcapped Himalayas, was crowded with divine beings. The great gods—Brahma, the Creator; Vishnu, the Preserver; and Śiva, the Destroyer—were lords of the mountain peaks. Their sublime power was like that of the sun, which could at once create with its warmth, preserve with its light and destroy with its scorching rays. Love, luck, fire, rain and all the other numberless elements of the universe were in the keeping of a myriad of lesser deities who lived in the shadows of the great gods' heavens.

The lower slopes of the mountains were home to Brahma's diverse and quarrelsome descendants, the godlings known as Asuras and Devas. The Asuras were creatures whose misshapen spirits had grown misshapen bodies. Tusked, horned and clawed, they had the torsos of men and the heads of beasts. In contrast, the finer-natured Devas loved the great gods and sought their blessing. The two races were perpetually at war.

But the poets told a tale in which all differences were subsumed, and gods, goddesses and demons made common cause. This is how it happened.

The drama occurred at a crucial juncture in time, at the moment when an old universe expired and a new one emerged from the void. After the all-encompassing sea had drowned the old world in one of its floodtides of destruction, the milky waters receded once again to reveal a land damp and new in the early light of the first day. Saffron flowers and pomegranate trees blossomed in fresh earth; bullock and human alike sniffed the sweet air that none had breathed before.

The great gods and their goddesses slept long on that first morning of new creation. Dawn itself was slow to wash the mountains, spilling from the arms of the morning goddess Ushas well past its appointed hour. High on Mount Meru, its pale light slipped through the thousand arched windows of the palace that crowned Brahma's paradise. The god of creation was sleeping beside his wife Sarasvati, the goddess of wisdom, whose beauty had caused Brahma's four heads to appear, allowing his gaze to dwell on every aspect of her loveliness.

On Mount Kailasa, dawn filtered into Śiva's heaven, casting rainbows in the mist above the waterfall of the mighty Ganges that plunged into the god's garden. The light played across the ascetic Śiva's sunken, unwashed features as he drowsed at his solitary meditations, and on the beautiful Parvati, still asleep in their marriage bed.

From the garden of Śiva and Parvati, the Ganges followed its course down to Vaikuntha, Vishnu's vast, divine city. The morning light sparkled on the domes of the golden temples that stretched for leagues across the mountains, and on the palace of the god rising in their midst. There, pillowed on a bed of crimson and indigo lotuses, Vishnu slept alone.

When the pale dawn warmed into the brilliance of day, the immortals stirred and rose at last, thirsty in the heat. Even in waking they were weary, and their thirst was not for the sweet, sacred water of the Ganges that flowed at their feet. On this first day of the new world, the gods and goddesses were weak for the want of amrita, their nectar, the essence of their strength and immortality.

In its last terrible flood, the primordial sea had swallowed all the precious possessions of the gods, and many of them— the celestial tree that granted all their wishes, the cow of plenty that provided for all their needs, the winged horse whose flight was faster than thought— had not emerged again with the reborn world. The amrita had dissolved into numberless droplets in the milky sea, which would not readily give it up.

On the slopes below the heavens, the godlings thirsted for the liquor, too, although they had never tasted it. Unlike the deities, the Devas and Asuras were mortal creatures, and in the battles between them, many on both sides perished. Because a single sip of the nectar would confer eternal life on the drinker, the Devas longed to be worthy of it as a gift from the great gods. The Asuras, however, had always sniffed about the gates of paradise, hoping to steal it.

Now there was no amrita to steal. Knowing they must pool their dwindling strength in order to recover it, the immortals decided to hold a council at Vish-

nu's palace. Brahma and Sarasvati climbed onto the back of their great silver-plumed swan, whose broad, beating wings lifted them into the sky. A jangling music floated up to them from the bells that garlanded the massive shoulders of Nandi, the white bull, carrying Śiva and Parvati along the cliffs. Below the peaks, where the rich colors of the newly made earth shimmered in the heat like a carpet freshly dyed and drying in the sun, they could see the multitudes of lesser gods following the path to Vaikuntha.

The deities met at the gates of Vishnu's palace. Inside, with his legs twisted into a lotus knot, the god sat atop the coiled serpent, Sesha, who served as his throne. One hand shielded his tired eyes from the glitter of his jeweled throne room, but he lifted his other three arms in a weary welcome to Śiva and Parvati, Brahma and Sarasvati, and all the divine company that came behind them. He too was pining for the sacred nectar.

With a series of muscular ripples that undulated like a current along his great length, Sesha rearranged his coils into a cluster of thrones for the great gods and goddesses. Leaning close together, they spoke of the precious liquor swirling in the vast ocean. It was there, yet so diluted that even divine eyes could not detect it. It would spill through the strongest fingers. Whispering almost to herself, Sarasvati called the nectar the cream of the milky sea.

Her words seemed to fill Brahma with a sudden energy. "The ocean is indeed a sea of milk," he declared, "and we will churn it. With a stick spun by a rope, we will make it render up its cream."

His companions were silent. The primordial sea was wider than the vast expanses of the Rajasthan desert and its depths could swallow up all the cities of humans and gods. Not even the tallest tree of the rainforest would be large enough to make a churning stick. Even the magical ropes of the divines that could rise from the ground by their own power would snap in the sea's currents.

But, Brahma explained, the churn would be of neither wood nor hemp. The gods would uproot Mount Mandara, a peak twenty-five thousand leagues high, and plant it in the sea bed as a churning stick. It would be turned not by a rope, but by the serpent-king Sesha, on whose coils they now rested.

The gracious serpent was willing to assist them and, even without the amrita, the strength of all the deities together was great enough to pry the mountain away from the earth. Yet, if the whole of the endless sea was to roil, the churning itself would require many more hands. All the godlings, Devas and Asuras alike, must be enlisted in the endeavor. The deities knew that help would only come from the Asuras at a price too high to bear: immortality for the wicked creatures. Therefore, they set themselves to be artful with the Asuras and ready with promises they would not keep.

Bearing Mount Mandara's weight on their shoulders, the immortals descended to the slopes of the godlings. When they heard great Brahma's plan for the churning, the fair young Devas volunteered their help. The Asuras too came forward, and demanded what the Devas only hoped for: a taste of the amrita as payment. The deities agreed to share the nectar among all the godlings.

In the middle of the sea, milk-white swells beat against the underbelly of the mountain as the gods lowered it into the water. League after league of mountain sank silently beneath the waves, but at last it settled with a shudder on the ocean floor. Wrapping his coils around the peak, Sesha offered his head to the Asuras and his tail to the Devas. The godlings took hold of the serpent and began to churn the sea of milk.

Mount Mandara spun first one way, then the other as the godlings hauled on the serpent-king. Stretched in agony, Sesha's breath blew hot and his eyes rolled back. With a hiss of effort, he tried to contain the hot venom that was bubbling up inside him, but when at last his fanged jaws opened, the poison sprayed from his mouth, rising high in an arc over the sea. Its mist spread like a bruise across the sky, carrying annihilation toward the shores of the world.

Śiva, lord of destruction, flung himself into the cloud. Terrible in garlands of skulls and cobras, spouting fire from his third eye, the god was death itself. The mist of venom was almost upon the mortal world when Śiva swallowed it.

His body contorted in a dance of pain, and his throat slowly darkened to a bloodless blue. Rushing to his side, Parvati

A winged wonder that bore the gods aloft

Haloed in glory, the god Vishnu and his consort Lakshmi rode through the skies on a mount that was itself a divinity, great in power and remarkable in form. The name of this being was Garuda. Its head, talons, beak and wings were those of an eagle, or—some said—a vulture; its limbs and trunk were of human shape. Garuda was of a size and strength unequaled: As the creature flew, the beating of its great wings caused the whole earth to wobble and overmastered the monsoon.

When not conveying the gods on their mysterious missions, Garuda skimmed low over the earth, hunting for sinners. With a thrust and snap of its beak, it would fall upon the wicked and devour them as if they were worms.

The nectar that gave
the Indian deities eternal youth
was lost in the waters
of the primeval sea. To retrieve it,
Brahma ordered that
the vast ocean be churned like
milk—using armies of
godlings, an uprooted mountain
and a sacred serpent
who offered himself as a rope.

caught him in a stranglehold. Her terror-hardened grip choked off the poison, sealing it in her husband's throat before it could flow through his whole body.

As the sky cleared, the pair returned to Mount Mandara to find that, where the spinning peak had risen loftily above the waves before, only its jagged crest was visible now. The mountain was sinking into the soft sea bed.

As Vishnu watched the waves closing over the peak, his fingers curled into webbed claws, and his back grew thick and hard. Like all the gods, he possessed a wardrobe of avatars, physical forms both human and animal, that he could assume at will. Becoming now the huge tortoise that was one of his avatars, the god dived into the sea. He burrowed beneath the mountain and supported it on his shell.

All the while, the godlings kept to their task, and soon the sea began to foam. Brahma glimpsed the horns of the cow of plenty swirling in the white water, and Sarasvati saw the branches of the wishing tree. The gods began to sing as the lost treasures appeared, and the godlings spun the mountain faster in time with their chanting. A froth whiter than the sea bubbled up in the eddies and washes of the churning. When a jeweled goblet broke the surface, the froth flowed into it. The amrita was restored.

Each deity drank deeply of the nectar. As its vigor flowed through them, their singing became shouting and laughter. Yet, when a last, unfamiliar shape appeared in the water, they fell silent.

A perfect lotus flower as large as a throne rose up through the waves. Seated on its petals was a goddess more beautiful than the blossom itself. At her appearance, said the poets, the sacred Ganges left its riverbed and flowed toward her to seek her blessing.

The Asuras howled and panted like the beasts they resembled when they saw her. Many clawed hands reached for her as she floated past, snatching at the hem of the damp sari that revealed even as it concealed her beauty. The goddess's eyes remained fixed on Vishnu, who was now restored to his divine form and refreshed by the life-giving powers of the amrita. Taking her hand, he drew her safely out of the Asuras' reach and was the first god to hear her whispered name, Lakshmi. Where she had come from, and who she was, remained a mystery.

Vishnu led Lakshmi into the protective coils of Sesha, now released from his labors. While the Asuras leered at her, Brahma tried to slip past them with the goblet of amrita. Its heady perfume wafted to their snouts, and they turned upon him, snatching the cup away.

At once, Vishnu transformed himself into an avatar of womanly beauty that rivaled Lakshmi. Dancing in among the Asuras, all winks and smiles, the temptress asked to be allowed to taste the first sip of the nectar. In a confusion of lust and thirst, they handed the goblet to the newcomer. She dissolved instantly into the triumphant Vishnu, who passed the cup to the Devas.

Swallowing the amrita at last, the Devas felt its power surge within them and knew that now they were immortal. The outraged growling of their half-brothers was drowned by the warcry of the Devas as they fell upon them. On the shore of the milk-white sea, the blood of the Asuras reddened the surf. Never falling in death, the Devas drove the still-mortal Asuras back from the shore to the rocky slopes of heaven. There, they cast every one of them over the cliffs to dwell in the sunless ravines and slime-washed caverns of the nether regions.

The Asuras fell long and far from the heavens, but the deities who watched their descent knew that the creatures were not yet vanquished. They would rule the lower world as powerful demons and wait for the chance to challenge the lords of the upper regions again.

Together, Vishnu and the goddess Lakshmi mounted the gold and crimson eagle Garuda and soared across the Himalayas to jeweled Vaikuntha. That night, among its many-colored lotus blooms, Vishnu did not sleep alone.

The whole world was suffused with the warmth of Vishnu and Lakshmi's ardor: Goddesses and gods embraced in their palaces, mortals cast longing glances at their partners, and the bird of paradise crooned ceaselessly to its mate. The air itself was charged with passion, and no one, divine or mortal, was immune.

But the storytellers recounted that one marriage languished for lack of sustenance even as other marriages were made: On Mount Kailasa, the goddess Parvati lay alone as she had done for more nights than she wished to remember. Sleep would not come to her. She heard the voice of her husband Śiva whispering in the garden outside her window. His words were not for her, nor for anyone. They were an endless litany of prayer in which he repeated the sacred syllables that held the concentrated wisdom of the scriptures. In his devotion to spiritual perfection, the Creator took nourishment only from prayer. He allowed himself no pleasure or comfort either from food, drink, music, dance or love.

Parvati tried to serve Śiva in his devotions, as a disciple might serve her master. Night after night, she went out into the midnight garden and kneeled beside him. In the moonlight reflected by the cascading Ganges, Śiva was as pale and still as a figure carved from ivory, his body smeared with the white ash of a thousand funeral pyres. Sometimes it seemed to Parvati that the god was stirring, and then she would lean close to him, but draw back in quick horror. The movement she perceived was not his at all, but the seething undulation of cobras winding themselves around his body and through his matted hair.

Parvati saw that Śiva wished to be left alone while he performed the rites of purification and sacrifice. When he turned away her ministrations, as he had turned away her love, Parvati wept bitterly. The other deities heard her suffering, but their thoughts were concentrated on the lower world. As the gods had foretold, the demons had grown from strength to strength. One bold nether Prince named Taraka, coveting the realm of the lesser divinities, had led his brothers in skirmishes along its borders.

The beleaguered godlings sent Indra, lord of rain, to ask great Brahma's help. Looking into his heart, where the future was written, the Creator said that a divine warrior as yet unborn would marshall a heavenly army to destroy Taraka. Indra asked when the godlings might look for this savior of their race, and Brahma told him that the wait might be long, for that future god of war was destined to be the son of Śiva and Parvati.

Indra feared for the godlings if they had to wait for Śiva's heart to warm by itself. He traveled, therefore, to a scented glade hung heavy with perpetual blossoms. Pairs of nesting birds and wild beasts with their mates stirred in the shadows as he passed. The glade was the home of Kama, god of love, his wife Roti, goddess of desire, and their companion Vasanta, the spirit of spring.

When Indra requested Kama to pierce Lord Śiva with an arrow of love, the handsome young god was afraid. Princes, priests, warriors and wise men all had fallen before his shafts, but to take aim at the destroyer god was a dangerous presumption. Still, Kama agreed to try, if Vasanta would accompany him.

Kama took his bow of sugarcane strung with a flight of honeybees and a quiver of his flower-tipped arrows. With Vasanta at his side, he stole into Śiva's garden, where the god sat in a trance of prayer. Parvati kneeled silently beside him. At Vasanta's approach, all the trees and flowers around them blossomed, startling the drowsy birds into sudden song. Śiva opened his eyes and, amid the sweet scents and sounds of unexpected spring, his gaze rested on Parvati's beauty as if for the first time.

Pulling himself sharply back to his meditation, Śiva closed his eyes again. Kama stepped from the trees and took aim. His bow bent and his arrow flew. Before it could reach its mark, however, the god's great third eye opened. It shot forth a bolt of fire that consumed both arrow and archer. Silently, Śiva rose and went from the garden, leaving Parvati and the terrified Vasanta, whose fear chilled the air and withered the new blossoms.

Then, as Kama's ashes blew around her, Parvati, too, left the icy garden. She did not follow her husband into his palace, but walked down from the domain of the gods toward the wilderness, knowing that Śiva's passion was only for prayer. If he wished to be alone, she would leave him absolutely alone. If asceticism was to be his only life, it would be hers also.

She wandered through many seasons of drought and rain. Her hair grew matted and her clothes fell into rags. She welcomed the pain of the rough earth tearing her hands and feet. She ate nothing and spoke only prayers.

One day, a beggar came upon Parvati as she chanted Śiva's name. In a voice full of mockery, he asked if she had sacrificed her youthful beauty for the god of destruction. When she nodded, the beggar laughed at her foolishness.

Śiva, he said, was a base lord who loved only death. The stench of burned flesh

Ignored by her ascetic mate, the goddess Parvati languished. But Śiva's attentions were
fixed on the infinite, distracted neither by her caresses nor by the snakes that nested in his hair.

clung to him, and his hair was matted with graveyard filth.

His words drowned her chanting. Finally, Parvati could stand no more. Crying that Śiva was her beloved lord, she started to turn away in despair. Suddenly, the beggar's face began to change, his features melting and shifting. His skin grew pale, and a third eye appeared in the middle of his forehead. His throat turned blue with the stain that had been caused so long ago by the serpent Sesha's venom. The beggar was Lord Śiva himself.

Before Parvati could kneel, the god dropped to his knees and took her hands in his. He told her that her spiritual strength had surpassed his own, for while she had lived far from home as a solitary wanderer, he had not been able to bear her loss. Parvati embraced him, saying that she had never truly been lost to him, and that the sacred word of her chanting had always been his name. So great was Śiva's joy that he instantly restored the spirit of the immolated Kama. Because his body had been destroyed, however, the god of love was destined to walk invisibly among mortals and immortals from that day forward.

Together, Śiva and Parvati returned to their paradise on Mount Kailasa where, before the next monsoon, she gave birth to Karttikeya, Śiva's son. Nursed by the Pleiades, stars that came down from the sky to suckle him, the child grew into the god of war. He possessed six heads and a dozen arms clutching various tools of destruction—rapiers, scimitars, daggers,

arrows and shields. With one of these weapons—the chroniclers left the details of the story cloudy—Karttikeya set upon and slew the demon Taraka, just as the old prophecies had promised.

Even a divinity dedicated to war could not rid heaven of all its enemies. Some demons seemed capable of outwitting or defeating all the gods. The tale was told of one Asura named Raktavira. To gain Brahma's favor, he had studied scriptures, prayed and fasted, and become more conscientious than any earthly priest or holy man in the practice of his devotions.

Through these exertions he had won from Brahma a promise that safeguarded him even against the god of war. By the Creator's leave, every drop of Raktavira's blood that spilled upon the ground would spring to life in the shape of a thousand demons. No one could challenge an enemy whose numbers would increase with every blow. Seemingly invulnerable, the demon brought misery to the lower regions of the world.

Parvati heard the lamentations of her worshippers suffering at the hands of Raktavira. She tasked Brahma to take back his boon, but he said he could not undo his own handiwork. Still, the cries from her temples below troubled the gentle-hearted Parvati, waking her from her sleep in Śiva's arms.

Anger at Raktavira grew in the goddess's breast, where only sweetness had been before. Her rage swelled into a powerful wrath, darkening her thoughts by day and invading her dreams at night. At last, when Parvati's tender flesh could no longer contain it, her fury took on a new integument, a terrible mantle of blood, sinew and bone. Black-skinned, long-tongued, four-armed, the goddess was the gentle Parvati no more. Her name was Kali, and she was bloodshed, pestilence, terror and death. From her forehead a third eye, like Śiva's, now glared. In this incarnation, she was indeed the true mate of the destroyer god.

Girding herself for war, Kali wrapped a garland of skulls still damp from the grave around her neck and a girdle of hands cut from human corpses around her waist. They were her only ornaments. She had no need of armor; she would dance naked into battle. With a sword in one hand and a dagger in another, Kali swept down from Mount Kailasa, calling Raktavira into the field. The demon came up the slope, eager to spill the unknown challenger's blood and not afraid of his own being shed, sure as he was of the promise that Brahma had made to him. At the sight of death-black Kali in the throes of battle-lust, her tongue writhing and her eyes rolling, he stopped.

She was upon him instantly. With two hands she caught him by the hair and swung him high off the ground, while in her other hands her sword and dagger flashed toward his throat. Raktavira hung helplessly in her grip, still unafraid, knowing that as his lifeblood spattered on the earth an army of demons would rise to destroy her.

Then, even as he felt the blades bite into his flesh, the demon saw Kali lean forward and open her mouth. As his blood spurted from the gashes toward her, she caught the steaming red stream between her lips. She swallowed long and greedily, her tongue snaking across her gory chin to catch every last drop. When at last Raktavira's wounds ran dry, she licked them clean, then flung his pale, drained corpse to the ground.

Although the lesser demons who had gathered to watch the battle scattered at her approach, Kali's many arms were everywhere, inescapable. Slitting throats and severing limbs, she drank their blood, too, even though it carried no magic threat. The blood tasted just as sweet and strong; it lightened her head and quickened her feet. Laughing and singing, she danced on the bodies strewn around her. For her partners, she whirled two dripping heads above her own.

Śiva watched the carnage from his heaven. Ferocity and bloodlust were his familiars, giving him strength whenever his own destructive powers were called upon by the gods. Yet he did not wish his consort to lose herself entirely in her frenzy and become only Kali, never Parvati again. Joining her on the blood-stained slope, he called out, saying the battle was over. Kali danced away from him, looking around wildly for more demons to slay. At last, Śiva waded into the gore and lay down among the bodies. Kali spun across the dead, leaping from corpse to corpse and finally landing on the god himself. Halting her dance abruptly, she stared down at him. The song of death

Why the patron of wisdom had a pachyderm's trunk

Ganesa, with his fat human body and elephant's head, was the Indian god of wisdom and success. A gluttonous fondness for the fresh fruit and rice cakes offered by his adoring followers gave him his potbelly. The origin of his elephant head was more mysterious, but one story explained it this way:

The goddess Parvati wanted a doorkeeper to protect her privacy in the bath. She blended dried skin from her body with magic unguents to form a living boy.

Assiduous in his duties, Ganesa refused entry even to Śiva, Parvati's husband, who one day in a fit of temper slashed off the boy's head. Overcome by remorse, Śiva took the head of the first creature he encountered and planted it on the child's shoulders. But in one sense, this proved a blessing for the boy. When he acquired an elephant's head, he also gained great virtue, for the noble beast was the embodiment of prudence, pity and sagacity.

83

died away. She kneeled and touched his face with a hand already turning pale. Śiva stood up and led Parvati away from the field of Kali's terrible triumph.

While the battles with Taraka and Raktavira bloodied the celestial foothills, another demon stood alone in the vastness of the Rajasthan desert, a living pillar of fire. Willing the sun to focus its brutal rays so intensely upon him that flames raced along his naked flesh and smoldered in his hair, the demon chanted an endless prayer to Brahma. His invocation rang in the god's ears for centuries, and for centuries, whenever the Creator cast his eyes across the oceans of sand, he saw the demon burning in the perpetual fire of his desert altar.

When he could ignore this living sacrifice no longer, the great god asked the demon what gift the heavens could bestow on him. The demon asked for those prizes of the gods, immortality and invincibility. After witnessing his supplicant's great courage in the flames, Brahma knew that he would be far too dangerous a threat to paradise if he possessed those qualities absolutely. He told the demon instead that the gifts would be his if he named one condition by which they could be lost. A voice from the flames answered that he would consent to lose in battle and die only by a woman's hand. Great Brahma nodded.

At once, the flames sank into the sand, revealing a massive creature snorting and tossing his head in triumph. Although his tall, broad body was thick with fat, he leaped powerfully from the altar onto the sand. With one muscled shoulder, he brushed Brahma aside like a bothersome fly. The god drew back from the touch of the coarse, hairy flesh and recoiled from the stableyard stench that clung to it. Brahma recognized him with disgust as Mahishasura, the nether lord who claimed a demon for his father and a she-buffalo for his mother.

Mahishasura scanned the desert horizon for the blue shadows of the Himalayas. Fixing his small, flesh-hidden eyes on the distant peaks, he set out across the wasteland, snorting and blowing. When he lumbered onto the heavenly slopes, he roared out his name and his challenge. Immortal and invincible, he would rule in this place, and the only answers to his cry were submission or death.

The demons slowly emerged from the netherworld and drew near, fearful of Mahishasura's rampant strength but uncertain of his proud talk. Impatiently, he caught one of the laggards and crushed him in his grip. The creature's desperate, dying blows with sword and dagger glanced harmlessly off a hide that was as thick as a buffalo's and, moreover, blessed by Brahma, god of all creation.

The other demons hurriedly joined ranks with Mahishasura, hailing him as their warrior-king and echoing his challenge to the gods. The temperamental rain-god Indra looked out from his mist-clad temple onto the field already swarming with demons. Taking up a long spike cut from a single diamond, he rushed out among them, enraged. His spike scattered the lesser demons, but

Kali, Queen of death and terror, adorned herself with severed heads to drink the blood of a victim and dance upon his corpse.

Mahishasura stood unmoved by its blows and struck back viciously at the god.

Exhausted, Indra withdrew and called on the great gods to come down from their heavens. On swan, bull and eagle, divinities arrived armed with discus and trident, bow and blade. Although they knew of Brahma's boon to the upstart demon, they threw themselves upon him. Using powers of illusion learned from his father, Mahishasura summoned a vision of a million selves to confuse his attackers. And with the brute muscle of his mother's kind, he bloodied Vishnu's eagle and stunned Śiva with a blow.

The buffalo-demon could not kill the immortals, but neither could they destroy him. At last, they wearied of the stalemate and retreated to the uppermost reaches of paradise. There, they pondered Brahma's boon. If only a woman could slay Mahishasura, then they must find a woman with the strength and courage to meet him in battle and defeat him: a divine woman. Brahma and Vishnu protested that Sarasvati and Lakshmi were too gentle-hearted for war, while Śiva was loath to call the bloody incarnation of Kali into being again.

Closing their eyes, they began to chant together in one voice, focusing the sacred power that was the wellspring of life, death and rebirth. As the chant swelled and soared across the mountaintops, a divine effulgence never seen before shone from the faces of the gods. Brahma's countenance glowed a burning crimson and Śiva's a brilliant white. The dark radiance of polished obsidian gleamed from Vishnu's face.

As the three streams of light crossed, the air itself shimmered in a dance of color. The hues merged and parted and merged again, slowly thickening into a pillar of light that hovered before the assembled gods. In its near-blinding brilliance, they perceived a face that held all the light and colors of the rainbow. Below it, the shining pillar molded itself into a graceful body as fine as an arrow and as taut as a bowstring.

It was the goddess Devi, newly born from the light of divinity, naked, smiling and proud, astride an enormous lion. She needed no words from the gods; she knew the battle she had been born to. Silently, Brahma laid his cloak of crimson silk across her shoulders, while Vishnu and Śiva placed in her twelve hands all the weapons of war they possessed.

Devi spurred her lion, which leaped down to the domain of Mahishasura in one great bound. On Vishnu's conch-shell trumpet, the goddess blew a note that shook the mountains and turned the winds from their course. Mahishasura, lodged in the demons' palace, started at the terrible noise and at the challenge he heard in it. He sent out a scout, who returned pale and trembling with the stammered message that a beautiful goddess had come to kill the buffalo-king.

Mahishasura laughed and commanded his minion to bring him this impudent young girl. He vowed that if she were as beautiful as she was spirited, he would marry her. But if she was less than perfect, she would die for her presumption.

When the scout hesitated, the demon-king roared loudly, mocking his servant's fear of a creature whose only weapons were smiles and blushes. He bade him take an army with him, if it would make the servant feel safer.

Eager for a look at her, a horde of lusty demon-soldiers rushed from the palace. As they approached, Devi sent a storm of spears and arrows into their midst and the earth ran dark with demons' blood. Then Devi's many arms were everywhere, piercing hearts and slitting throats. As the demons fell, her lion devoured them. Soon, the battlefield was silent except for the crunch of bones between the great cat's jaws. Only one demon, bloody and exhausted, remained alive. Devi sent him back to Mahishasura, saying again that she had come to kill him. Since she did not relish inflicting death, however, she would spare his life if he would retreat to the underworld.

Mahishasura hardly noticed the loss of his army, so stirred was his brute's blood by the thought of a mate. The battered survivor's account of the goddess's beauty in battle only roused him more. Once again calling upon his father's teachings, he transformed himself into a shape designed to please a lovely girl. Shedding his thick buffalo hide and rough-hewn features, Mahishasura turned into a fine-boned youth with golden skin and almond eyes. He went out in search of Devi, another legion of demons at his heels.

He found her on the battlefield and her loveliness was greater than he had imagined. He did not know many sweet words, but he kneeled and said them all. Devi, who could see the buffalo inside the youth, stood silent while his words washed over her. Then, with only a sigh of impatience as a warning, she struck him full in the face with Śiva's trident.

Roaring with pain, Mahishasura forgot his desire and took the form of a lion to attack her. When Devi's blade proved swifter and sharper than his great claws, the demon took on an elephant's body to crush his foe. Devi's shield was too strong, however, and he became at last a buffalo. Lowering his horned brow, he charged the goddess.

One of Devi's hands held a victory goblet, and she raised it to him now with a smile. When the beast was almost upon her, she threw back her head and drank. With another hand, she hurled her discus at his throat and severed his head. She lifted her cup again, heavenward, in salute and farewell to the gods. Then, with a promise to return if ever they had need of her, Devi vanished.

In paradise, all the immortals rejoiced in a festival of triumph. Beneath parasols spangled with mirrors and beads, the goddesses painted their hands and faces with filigrees of vermilion flowers, while the gods donned garlands of lotuses. As they dined on sweetmeats and honeyed fruits, the music of flutes, bells, cymbals and drums flowed all around them. Soon its rhythm spun them in a dance. In the whirl of their footsteps, blossoms of fig and jasmine blew down from heaven and covered the bloodstained battlefields of gods and demons with flowers.

It was decreed that only a woman could slay Mahishasura, a shape-shifting monster
who menaced the universe. Therefore Brahma, Vishnu and Śiva together created
the twelve-armed goddess Devi, who rode into battle on a lion and destroyed him.

A Tale of Radiance Reborn

When the world was first formed, said the scholars of old Japan, the finer elements rose to become heaven, while the base matter took the shape of earth. The two realms were, by their very nature, separate: Trouble and confusion ensued when they came together. Never was this truth brought home more clearly than in a violent encounter between the sun-goddess Amaterasu, first among heaven's eight hundred deities, and her impetuous, earthbound brother, the sea-ruler and storm-god Susano.

As long as the siblings dwelled apart, heaven and earth basked in Amaterasu's radiance, and all creation flourished. But Susano coveted his sister's glory. Seething restlessly in the lower realm, he determined to claim a place in heaven.

So a time came when Amaterasu, serene on the celestial heights, heard a rumbling and quaking from below. Apprehensively, she fitted an arrow to the string of the bow she kept with her to ward off intruders. When, heralded by thunderclaps and the crashing of rocks, the swarthy storm-god finally appeared before her, she raised the weapon in fear.

Weary and unkempt after his long climb, Susano was a terrible sight; sweat ran down his cheeks and matted his beard, and his eyes glittered like shafts of lightning.

Amaterasu would have ordered her brother back to his own domain, but she knew his fierce temper and the chaos he could cause when roused to anger. Instead she quietly asked him the business that had brought him from his home. He came with a challenge, he replied. Was not his divinity as great as hers? Let them test their powers of creation one against the other. If he, Susano, could match his sister's feats, then he too should have a place beside her up on high.

Amaterasu feared to provoke his wrath with a refusal. So she agreed to the contest, but cunningly disarmed him by asking for his sword as an instrument to work her wonders on. Gripping it in both hands, she snapped it into three pieces across her knee, then opened her mouth and swallowed the fragments. When her lips parted again, she exhaled a fine mist, and from this mist tumbled three plump infant goddesses.

Now it was Susano's turn. He asked for the jeweled necklace that sparkled around Amaterasu's neck. This he bit between his teeth until it cracked apart, and spit out five fragments as if they were nutshells. Then he too exhaled a vapor. This time the mist gathered into the forms of five infant gods.

Susano could not contain his pride. Stamping the ground, he bellowed his joy, then rushed off to boast of his victory. Amateratsu took the baby deities out of harm's way and returned home, fearing the consequences.

Her misgivings were soon justified. Careering across the heavenly plains, Susano caused the banks of irrigation ditches to cave in and a great wave of floodwater to surge forth. A herd of wild ponies stampeded in terror across the rice fields, destroying the newly planted crop. Trees were uprooted and raucous birds wheeled high in the air, searching in vain for somewhere to alight.

With every passing hour, messengers hurried to Amateratsu's door with new reports of havoc. The storm-god had shattered the pillars of holy temples, he had trampled the sacred gardens to mud and left excrement in the shrines. His booming laughter created typhoons.

Finally, shamed by his defiance of her authority, Amateratsu sought refuge in a deep cave and blocked the entrance with a heavy boulder.

Now the source of all the world's light was blotted out, heaven and earth were plunged into darkness. Order and harmony were turned upside down: All living things began to wither and die, and wickedness flourished in perpetual night. Racked by despair, and knowing that only the sun-goddess Amateratsu could save them from chaos, the gods assembled to decide what must be done.

Many schemes were put forward and rejected before a plan was finally agreed upon. Amateratsu could not be forced from her hiding-place; she must be tempted out. So it was decided to stage a great festivity outside the cave where she

hid, with all the gods in attendance. Metalworkers were instructed to forge a marvel never before seen: a bronze disk so smooth that any image caught in its reflection would be cast back at the beholder. The goddess Uzume, guardian of the mysteries of the sacred Mount of Kagu, agreed to perform a dance. And all the cockerels of heaven were collected together to crow for the sun's return.

Before the mouth of Amaterasu's cave, the trees and bushes were festooned with strings of jewels that winked and glittered in the light of colored lanterns. There, when all the gods were gathered, Uzume began her performance.

Wearing only a flimsy gown of bamboo grass gathered on the sacred mountain and held together by a slender sash, the goddess danced barefoot on an upturned tub. Her rhythm was that of the earth itself, the sinuous movements of her legs and arms imitating the rise of new life from its hidden seed. Faster and faster she turned, louder and louder her feet hammered on the tub, until her clothing came undone and only a handful of leaves still clung to her glistening brow. The gods shouted and cheered as she spun in the flickering lamplight, and the cockerels, roused from their torpor, began to crow as though at break of day.

Lying dejected in her cave, the drowsy Amaterasu heard faint echoes of the tumult. In a world subdued by darkness, what could cause such high spirits? Someone outside nudged the boulder and she peered through the chink.

The very first thing her eyes fell upon was the bronze mirror, held by a waiting

attendant, and her own likeness cast back from it. She saw long black hair and limpid eyes—features she remembered from the dim reflections seen in ponds and the waters of deep streams. Yet the face now looked drawn and haggard. Shocked, she stepped forward from the cave. Instantly a waiting god slid behind her to block a retreat. And as Amaterasu hesitated, cut off from her refuge, her light once again flooded the heavenly plains, and the eight hundred deities bowed low in submission.

The deities next sought out Susano and banished him from heaven forever. Before he left for the lower realms, his beard was cut off and the nails of his fingers and toes were clipped so he could not rend or claw the skin of the earth or the flesh of its creatures.

Tranquility and fruitfulness returned to all creation, nourished once more by the generative powers of the sun-goddess. It was as though nothing had ever changed, though there was one significant difference. Eight new godlings graced the heavenly realm, and in times to come each of them would found noble dynasties: From the eldest male among them, the royal line of the Emperors of Japan would one day spring.

Odin, chieftain of the war-loving gods named the
Aesir, battled giants, seduced mortals and woke the dead in
his quests for occult wisdom and absolute power.

Four

Prideful Rulers
of the Elder World

On the cold fringes of northern Europe, Norse bards once sang of a vanished tribe of gods and goddesses. The tale they wove was as harsh and turbulent as the north itself.

In those regions, nature was a tyrant. Wind and wave lashed the offshore skerries and carved the cliffs into fanged grotesqueries. Gales churned whirlpools among the coastal rocks, and mists rolled inland from the fjords like phantom armies on the march. In the gloom of the primeval forests, wolves, bears and cold-blooded serpents ruled.

Every settlement had its storytellers in those days, and they looked backward to a universe that existed before our own. It was inhabited by a populous pantheon of deities, as well as giants, dwarfs, elves, wild beasts and humans.

Each race occupied its own territory. The gods' home, Asgard, was a fortress set on a high crag at the earth's center. A bridge in the form of a rainbow linked Asgard to Midgard, the land of humankind. Midgard, in turn, was surrounded by a vast ocean; its far shores bounded the wasteland of Jötunheim, domain of the giants. And below all these realms lay subterranean Niflheim, the province of the dead. Yet there would come a time when all would be swallowed up in a war that shattered the cosmos.

The bards pieced together the history of this lost world from fragments: old songs, riddles, scraps of prophecy, portions of half-forgotten epics in prose or rhyme, runic symbols carved on flat-faced stones. The tale they told was a saga of torture, rape and sorcery, of falsehood and duplicity, of lust for gold and power, of wars waged with weapons and wars waged with magic spells. Its heroes—and its villains—were the members of a large and many-branched family of gods known as the Aesir, and the otherwordly beings that shared their shining universe.

Unlike the divinities who inhabited the slopes of Mount Olympus, dwelling eternally in their sunny vineyards and olive groves, or the sensuous deities of the oriental lotus-lands, the Norse gods were not immortal. Indeed, some sages claimed they were no more than ancient human Kings, who had come roaring out of the east in a storm of gore and glory.

Wishing to defy death, the Aesir contrived to prolong their lives indefinitely. They had obtained, from sources unknown, a stock of magic apples. Whenever they began to age or sicken, they ate of this sacred fruit and at once regained their strength and youth.

But the Aesir could not conquer mortality forever. The fate of all living creatures, and of the world itself, lay in the hands of three female beings so powerful that the name of goddess scarcely did them justice. These were the Norns, three sisters who wove the webs of doom and wrote the books of destiny.

The Norns clustered around every infant's cradle to decree its future, and appeared at every deathbed to sever the thread of life. So, too, had they gathered at time's beginning, to sing the doom of the gods themselves. The fate they foretold was this: Despite all their wisdom, their powers, their mastery of magic, the Aesir were to be destroyed, and the reason for their undoing would be their own corruption.

No sage could say for certain precisely when the downfall of the gods began. It may have been the day when the Aesir conspired to cheat one of the giants.

There was little love lost between Asgard and Jötunheim. Gods and giants had fought many bitter wars, and even when peace prevailed, all encounters between them were fraught with suspicion. Yet the two races bartered and traded, and their bloodlines often mingled, in spite of the fact that the giants were of prodigious size and the gods only slightly larger than ordinary humankind.

During one of the times of truce, a giant, mounted on a drayhorse, entered Asgard in the murk of a midwinter morning. Even if Heimdall, sentinel of the gods, had not blown his horn, the Aesir would have known of the visitor's arrival. His footsteps shook the earth, and the rainbow bridge leading into Asgard quivered under his weight.

One by one, the Aesir emerged from their dwellings to investigate: Odin, the father and chieftain of the clan; his consort Frigg, who had the power to read the future but never spoke of what she saw; Thor, god of war and hurler of thunderbolts, armed with the great hammer that helped him maintain order in the universe; countless others, goddesses and gods alike, stood shivering in air so cold it turned their spoken words to ice.

Odin asked the giant his business. Diffident despite his size, the giant lowered his eyes, shuffled his rough sandals, and muttered that he had heard that the Aesir were looking for a master builder.

Odin said that this was so. They wished to construct a wall around Asgard. The giant raised hands with fingers thick and gnarled as ancient oaks. He was, he claimed, the best workman in Jötunheim. No matter how big a rampart the gods wanted, he could build it faster and better than anyone in the universe.

Odin looked him up and down. He asked the giant what fee he had in mind. The giant was not interested in gold or

A triad of divinities older than time, the Norns
were skilled at weaving. But their cloth was the web of fate;
once woven, no power could alter its pattern.

silver. It seemed the Aesir had something else he wanted. He scanned the cluster of goddesses looking on. He desired, he said, a woman of Asgard for his bed. That was his price; he was not prepared to bargain.

The Aesir withdrew to confer among themselves. Soon Odin returned with a proposition. If the giant completed the rampart before the winter was over, he would have any goddess of his choosing as a bride. But there was one condition: He had to do the work alone, without the aid of henchmen or helpers. And if there was even a single stone missing from the wall on the first day of spring, the gods would pay him nothing.

Odin barely concealed his amazement when the giant agreed to the bargain, asking only that he be permitted to use his horse for hauling and carrying. Odin consented. Not even a giant could complete a wall of the desired dimensions in the time allowed. Asgard's womankind seemed in little danger.

The Aesir's complacency faded, however, when they saw the giant's horse at work. The stallion flew up the mountainsides, seemingly unaware of the slabs of rock on the sledge behind it. The bulwark appeared to be building itself, growing higher by the hour.

The giant paused from time to time to squint up at the watery February sun, and to leer at the goddesses who came to watch him as he worked. Regretting the bargain, the Aesir sought a way to slow the giant's progress. They would much rather be left with a half-finished wall than see one of their Princesses forced to suffer the rough embraces of such a churl.

They consulted Loki, master of mischief. It was not certain that Loki was a god at all; some folk said that giant's blood ran in his veins. His favorite games were shape-shifting and falsehood. Murder seemed but a sport to him, and his progeny were monsters. He was father to the Fenris wolf, an enormous beast that was kept in chains below the earth. It had been prophesied that this creature would someday break free of its fetters, signaling the end of the world.

Despite his threatening offspring, Loki was tolerated by the Aesir, who found him useful. The Aesir never needed to stain their own hands with dishonest or ignoble acts: Loki did their dark work for them.

Now they called upon Loki to help them out of their troubles. He obliged by shifting shape and gender, transforming himself into a mare. The creature turned its hindquarters toward the stallion and twitched its tail in delicate invitation. As anticipated, the stallion at once abandoned its labors and galloped off after the female. But the giant did not accept this setback with good grace. Aware that he had somehow been cheated, he ran amok through Asgard.

Only Thor could stop the raging colossus. He flung his hammer. With a thunderclap, the weapon pierced the giant's skull. Lightning flashed from ears and eyeballs before the massive head split in two. The body fell with a crash that

The Norse deities were vulnerable to the corruptions
of the flesh and the ravages of time. They knew how to
forestall death, but not to conquer it.

was heard as far away as the giant's own land of Jötunheim. The blood that was pouring from the wound flooded the streets of Asgard, and it took one hundred slaves, straining and heaving with ropes and drayhorses, to drag the corpse away.

The giant's stallion had vanished, but eleven months later, the mare that had distracted it reappeared in Asgard, ready to drop a foal. The Aesir looked on as the beast gave birth. What they saw amazed them. The offspring was an enormous, eight-legged colt. A greater shock was yet to come. Before their wondering eyes, the steaming, sweating flanks of the mare melted away, to reveal Loki himself, doubled up with laughter.

With a deep bow, he presented the newborn creature to Odin. Loki promised that it would grow into the greatest horse the world had ever seen.

The chroniclers did not relate what revenge, if any, the giants took on the Aesir. The gods of Asgard were soon occupied with troubles on another front: Civil war was brewing in heaven.

The Aesir did not rule the world alone. Another tribe of gods, the Vanir, lived outside the boundaries of Asgard, and concerned themselves with fertility, corn and the tilling of the soil, matters which were of small interest to Odin and his court. The two groups coexisted, warily but without direct conflict, until the day when a Vanir priestess was made to suffer an outrage in Odin's hall. She was a goddess of sorcery and treasure: Indeed, her name, Gullveig, meant "Lust for Gold." The reason for her visit was not recorded, nor why she came unguarded and alone to a territory that she knew was less than friendly.

Gullveig entered Odin's court arrayed in emeralds and rubies; her slender arms and neck were encircled with bands of gold. The glitter of her ornaments was outshone only by the rapacious gleam in the eyes of her hosts.

Her arrival had interrupted a raucous feast; she was offered a seat, although not in a place of honor, and the revelry resumed. As the mead flowed, the Aesir began to shed their decorum, and forgot the courtesies that were owed to a guest. One of the gods sidled up to Gullveig and fingered the intricate brooch on her tunic; another reached out, grabbed her arm, and sank his teeth into a bracelet to see if the gold was real.

Gullveig rose from her bench and strode up the hall to complain to her host of this treatment. But before she reached Odin, someone thrust out a foot and sent her flying. Not only did the chieftain of the Aesir condone these liberties, he laughed to see her sprawled out on the floor among the rushes, with the dogs sniffing around her legs.

The sight of Gullveig's humiliation unleashed something even more terrible in Odin's followers. They fell upon her, dragged her to the great hearth at the center of the hall, and tore the finery off her back. Then they kicked aside the slaves who were roasting an ox over the fire, pulled away the meat, and lashed

Master of thunderbolts, Thor was the lord of war
and justice. In his charge lay the order and harmony of the
universe; without his vigilance, all would be chaos.

the screaming Gullveig to the iron spit. Laughing, they pierced her with their own spears and watched the blood ooze and drip, hissing, into the fire. The stench of burnt flesh filled the hall as a pack of slaves fought among themselves over Gullveig's garments.

The chroniclers offered no explanation for the gods' outrageous act. But there were those among the Aesir who had long desired an opportunity to goad the Vanir into outright war. And there were some in Asgard whose lust was roused by the act of inflicting pain.

Yet the roars torn from Gullveig's throat were cries not of agony but of fury. The heat of the flames and the heat of her anger split her asunder. Something that was no longer Gullveig emerged from the charred flesh.

The throng around the fire parted. A creature with empty eyes and blood-black mouth rushed past them and vanished from the hall. For a long time, no one knew what became of her. But the poets later revealed that she would reappear as Heid, sibyl and spellspinner, mother and mentor of all witches. The Aesir were destined to meet her again, in very different circumstances. That was still far in the future, however.

News of the atrocity traveled swiftly back to the Vanir. The crime against Gullveig could not go unpunished. Soon a delegation of Vanir stormed into Odin's hall, demanding blood money. It was the law of the north: Those who killed or injured were obliged to pay reparations to their victim's family. Refusal to do so was tantamount to a declaration of war.

The Aesir had tasted blood, and liked it. They were spoiling for a fight. The emissaries went home empty-handed.

The conflict that followed was long and bitter. At times the Vanir seemed to be winning, then the Aesir snatched the advantage. The Vanir often resorted to witchwork and battle magic to turn the tide in their favor, and Asgard's forces summoned their own sorceresses to retaliate in kind. In the end, weary of war, the two parties secured a truce by the exchange of hostages. Gods from each side went to live among their former enemies as guarantors of peace.

Two who went from Asgard to dwell among the Vanir were Hoenir, handsome but dull-witted, and Mimir, the sage of the Aesir, wiser even than Odin. Impressed by Hoenir's fine looks and noble mien, the Vanir heaped honors upon him, and invited him to sit at all their councils and deliberations.

Sometimes Mimir accompanied Hoenir to these congresses and found opportunities to whisper words of wisdom in his ear, helping him to give a good account of himself and arrive at the right decisions. But whenever Mimir was absent, Hoenir became flustered and foolish. If he was asked for his opinion on matters of import, he hedged and prevaricated, refusing to commit himself.

The Vanir grew daily more suspicious. They had dispatched the best of their race to be pledges in Asgard. Had the

Freya, goddess of fertility, came to live as a
hostage among the Aesir after their bitter wars with an alien
pantheon. Cats were her symbols and familiars.

Aesir sent them this weak-minded creature as an insult?

Instead of taking out their anger on Hoenir—who was beneath contempt—they turned their attention to his mysterious companion. The gods did not deal in soft words. The message that they conveyed to the Aesir was unequivocal: It consisted of the still-bleeding head of Mimir, wrapped in a sack.

The chroniclers did not explain why the Aesir let this violent act go unchallenged. Perhaps they were too tired of battle; perhaps they admitted to themselves that Hoenir had not done their ancient race credit as a hostage. But it was not in their interests to upset the precarious balance of power, nor imperil the great treaty that was even then being negotiated with the Vanir.

Odin received Mimir's head in silence. He dismissed all his companions and carried the stained bundle to a place known only to himself. There, he bathed the head with oils that would preserve it without taint, and rubbed the flesh with herbs and powdered roots, all the while murmuring incantations.

Then he set the head upright, surrounded it with flickering candles, and waited. In time, as Odin expected, the eyelids snapped open, and dead Mimir smiled at him. Odin whispered a question; Mimir answered.

Never did Odin reveal the content of their discourse. But it became known in Asgard that Odin took counsel from Mimir's own lips, just as he had done in the sage's lifetime. Preserved by Odin's spells

and drugs, the head lived on. Odin consulted it many times thereafter.

Despite the slaying of Mimir, a permanent peace was finally reached between Asgard and the Vanir. To mark the treaty, the members of both clans spit into a great caldron. From these mingled waters, the gods created Kvasir, the wisest, most learned mortal ever to live. No question was too deep for him, no subject too esoteric, no riddle too obscure.

Ḣe traveled the world to impart his knowledge to all humankind, but his journey came to a sudden and violent end at the hands of a pair of malevolent dwarfs. Luring him away from a feast on some pretext, they murdered Kvasir and drained his blood into two stone crocks and an iron kettle. Then they mixed this vital sap with honey and hid it away in a warm place to ferment into mead.

When the Aesir came looking for Kvasir, his killers told them that the scholar had become so engorged with learning that he had choked on it and died before their eyes. The gods went away disconsolate, while the dwarfs stole back to the storehouse to chortle over their possession of a liquor that was the distillation of all poetry and wisdom.

But they did not keep this mead to themselves for long. By a circuitous route which entailed death, duplicity and the payment of ransoms, the precious mead passed into the hands of a cave-dwelling giant named Suttung. News of the mead reached the ears of Odin, who craved knowledge as a drunkard craves wine.

To obtain the liquor, the god disguised himself as an itinerant laborer and went down into the land of the giants. As if by chance, he ambled into a meadow belonging to Suttung's brother, where nine slaves were mowing hay. He listened to the thralls cursing as they attempted to carry out their task with blunt, rusty scythes. Then he offered to sharpen their tools with the hone that hung at his belt. Once treated, the implements sliced through the tough grass as if cutting through butter.

Odin said he might be persuaded to sell the hone. The men argued among themselves over who should have it. Odin tossed the sharpener into the air and the thralls scrambled to catch it as it fell. In the ensuing struggle, all nine of them died, butchered by one another's scythes.

Odin then proceeded at a leisurely pace to the farmhouse to present himself as an innocent stranger in search of shelter. There he found Suttung's brother, gnashing his teeth and tearing his hair. The giant had just learned that all his slaves were dead. Who now would tend his fields and bring in the crops?

The traveler remarked that he could easily do the work of all nine thralls. He asked only the most modest of wages in return. For a drink of Suttung's celebrated mead, he would bend his back and toil in the fields all summer long. The giant hedged. He had no access to his brother's store of mead, but if the stranger worked well for him all season, he would do his best to obtain some of the magic brew.

Odin consented. With the strength of nine men and the will of nine hundred, he completed all the tasks on the giant's farm. He tended the livestock, mowed the meadows and bound the sheaves of hay, cleared new ground with hoe and shovel, carried stones to mark the boundaries, and slept at night on a bench near his master's fire.

When the season's work was done and the harvest safely gathered in, Odin reminded his employer of their bargain. Together they went to Suttung's subterranean hall, where the farmer asked his brother for a cup of mead to pay the worker's wages. Scowling, Suttung refused to give so much as a drop away.

Odin was undaunted. He lingered unnoticed in the giant's busy household. He chose his moment, then sidled up to Suttung's daughter Gunnlod, and charmed her with sweet words. Soft and subtle was the wooing style of Asgard in comparison with the coarse approaches of amorous giants; Gunnlod was captivated by the stranger and led him to her bed.

For three days and nights they dallied together, and on each night Odin succeeded in persuading his paramour to let him drink deep of the magic mead. On the third night, he drained all the vessels dry. Then, without a word of farewell to Gunnlod, he transformed himself into an eagle and flew away, bearing within himself the essence of poetry.

Suttung, alerted by the lamentations of his daughter, used his own occult power to acquire eagle's wings and flew off after the thief. Pursuer and pursued sped over Jötunheim, their wingbeats resounding like thunder. But Odin's sorcery was the stronger. He evaded the giant and reached Asgard safely.

The gods had learned of Odin's quest for the mead. When they saw him approaching, still in the form of an eagle, they set out vats, and into these Odin spit the precious liquor. According to some scribes, a few drops of the mead fell outside Asgard's walls, to become the source of inspiration for earthly poets.

The bards who drank this precious essence used their gifts to praise one god above the rest. This was Balder, son of Odin, embodiment of all graces and virtues, loved by the Aesir and adored by mortals. But gruesome nightmares haunted Balder and woke him screaming. He could barely bring himself to recount the horrors that loomed up in these nocturnal visions, but goddesses wise in such things whispered that the dreams were portents of violent death. The Aesir consulted a witch, who uttered terrible warnings and incomprehensible messages.

The gods met in council. They could not imagine anyone—or anything—who could possibly wish ill on their beloved Balder, but nevertheless they would take all necessary measures to protect him. It was agreed that every creature or object capable of inflicting pain or injury should be made to swear a vow, promising that they would never harm the shining god.

The poets averred that on the day of the great oath-taking, all the creatures and substances in the world were given voice and language. The spirits that animated fire and water swore upon the golden arm-ring of Frigg that they would not burn or drown her son. Snakes vowed not to bite him; metals agreed not to cut his flesh; stones would not strike him; trees would never lend their limbs as arrow shafts or cudgels. Even the illnesses that plagued the flesh swore not to infect him. Poisonous plants declared that they would never burn his entrails, nor pollute his blood. Every conceivable source of danger made the compact.

Once reassured, the gods' mood lightened. They made a sport of Balder's inviolability. Laughing and joking, they cast stones at him, tossed knives and firebrands, secure in the knowledge that none of these could hurt him. But Loki, who loathed Balder's virtue as much as he envied his invulnerability, was less amused. He wove a plot.

All unaware, the goddess Frigg gave an audience to a visitor. She welcomed a young woman who came to ask, as one mother to another, how Frigg had rendered her precious son so safe from harm. Odin's Queen told the tale of the great oath-taking. But she admitted that she had exempted one tender shoot from the command. There was a slender mistletoe growing out of an oak tree west of her palace. It was so young and fragile that she believed it incapable of injury.

The visitor pondered for a moment, changed the subject, exchanged a few

Consort of Odin and powerful mother-goddess
in her own right, Frigg was patroness of marriage and fecundity.
She rode in a chariot drawn by sacred rams.

pleasantries, and departed. Once out of sight of Frigg's palace, Loki stepped out of this feminine disguise.

That night was Midsummer Eve—the time when the light never faded from the sky. Asgard rang with the noisy revelry of the gods, celebrating the great fire festival that marked this high point of the year. The mead and barley beer was flowing too fast and the drinking horns were upended too often for any of the Aesir to notice that one member of their company had slipped away. A little to the west, in the silent grove illumined by the pale rays of the midnight sun, a figure stood below the mistletoe-bearing tree, then hurled up a volley of stones to knock the young plant out of the oak.

The next morning, Loki made his way to the place of parliament. He saw the other gods joking with Balder, shooting him with spears and arrows that bounced harmlessly off his flesh. Only Hoder, Balder's blind brother, stood apart from this sport. Because of his affliction, the game had no meaning for him. Loki wandered nonchalantly up to Hoder. He remarked upon the good humor and fine appearance of all the Aesir on this midsummer day, dwelling with particular enthusiasm on the beauty of Hoder's sister-in-law, Nanna, Balder's wife.

This was a sore point for Hoder, and Loki knew it. Long years before, the two brothers had quarreled over the hand of the fair Nanna. In the battle they fought for possession of her, Balder had won the lady and Hoder had lost his sight. It was a pity, mused Loki, that Hoder could not join in the general merriment of throwing things at Balder. He suggested that perhaps he himself could act as Hoder's eyes, guide his hand and help him to play the game with the others.

Loki slipped something into the blind god's grasp: a mistletoe branch with a sharpened tip. Hoder took hold of the shaft, cocked an expert ear to determine precisely where the living target stood, and threw the mistletoe. It pierced Balder's body, even as a peal of laughter rose in the young god's throat.

The horror of that moment reverberated through all the worlds, for he was the gentlest and kindest of the gods. Now he was gone, the radiance of his life quenched in an instant.

The Aesir began preparations for the funeral. There was much to be done. Someone reached out a hand to close Balder's lips and eyelids. A fragment of cloth—torn, perhaps, from the skirts of Nanna, his grieving wife—was placed over his head. Slaves carried the body away to wash and anoint it, and the order went out immediately to the most skillful spinners, weavers and seamstresses of Asgard to create the fairest, finest garments that eyes had ever seen.

Meanwhile, the Aesir prepared Balder's own longship to carry him out of the world of the living. It was a noble craft, as beautiful as its lost master, its twin prows curled into serpents' tails. Along the keel, carved warriors thrashed in the twisting coils of wooden,

Sometimes shunned and sometimes exploited by
the Aesir, the trickster Loki roamed the worlds of mortals,
gods and spirits, sowing mischief and disharmony.

dragons, and sculpted monsters of unknown species thrust their heads out of the timbers, fore and aft. Now it lay, uncaptained, in the harbor.

The members of Balder's household brought his most prized possessions to stock the vessel for its final journey. Bronze spears and gold-hilted swords, a battle-ax adorned with acanthus leaves traced out in silver wire, a jeweled riding harness, dragon-headed arm rings, giant drinking horns—all these splendors and more besides were loaded on board. Nanna stood on deck, supervising every detail to satisfy herself that her husband would want for nothing on his voyage to the land of the dead.

When the ship was ready, the body of Balder was carried to a canopied bier amidships. With her own trembling hands, Nanna fastened shoes of reindeer skin on Balder's feet, that he might walk among the dead with grace and comfort. Platters piled high with fruit and herbs were placed beside him, alongside pitchers of mead to slake his thirst. His favorite horse was led onto the ship and slaughtered, and a pair of fine white milch cows were similarly sacrificed.

The gods gathered on the shore. Odin and his consort Frigg came forward, escorted by a retinue of ravens. Freya, the goddess of love and beauty, arrived in a chariot drawn by cats. Her brother Frey, lord of peace and prosperity, rode in one pulled by a golden-bristled boar. All the deities brought their own gifts and mementos to lay upon the pillow of their lost brother. Only blind Hoder was absent,

scarcely able to believe that his own hand had struck the deathblow.

The men's knotted muscles gleamed with sweat as they struggled to drag the great vessel along the beach. But the weight of the hull, laden with gravegoods and the gods' own parting gifts, was too much for them. They gave up and collapsed, exhausted, upon the shore.

Because the strength required was beyond them, the Aesir dispatched a messenger to the land of the giants, and a giantess soon appeared to complete the task. She came riding on a wolf, reined by living serpents. With a single heave, she sent the vessel into the sea, and the whole earth shook.

Yet one thing remained to be done before the funeral ship was put to the torch. Balder required a servant to accompany him in death. According to the custom of the northlands, the attendant had to be a female servant from the dead man's household, and one who freely offered up her life for love of her master.

The gods looked toward the huddled slaves, to see which of them would come forward. A black-shawled maid stepped forth, but Nanna flung out an arm and blocked her path: "Balder will take no serving-wench," she said. At this, the gods murmured, uneasy. The practice was an ancient one, not lightly breached.

But the moment had come. The tide was on the turn. It was time for Balder to sail to the netherworld in his ship of flame. At the water's edge, Balder's widow cast the first torch to ignite her husband's pyre. The rest of the Aesir hurled their firebrands. When the ship was ablaze, Nanna flung herself into the inferno.

The gods well understood her despair. Without Balder, their whole world grew darker. Time did nothing to heal the pain of their bereavement. Eventually they resolved to send a messenger to the subterranean goddess, Hel, Queen in the land of the dead. Her realm was so populous, the Aesir reasoned, that she might be willing to accept a ransom and release a single one of her captives.

Hermod, a son of Odin, volunteered to seek his brother in the underworld. He borrowed his father's charger, the eight-legged Sleipnir, to make the journey. For nine days and nights, Hermod galloped through empty valleys, meeting no one, hearing nothing but the echo of his horse's hooves. Then he came to a bridge, roofed with golden thatch, that spanned a dark river.

A maiden stood there as sentry. It was her task to count the dead when they crossed over. She told Hermod she had indeed seen Balder pass. Following the road she showed him, Hermod came to a pair of tall iron gates. He dug his spurs into Sleipnir's flanks, and the steed flew up and over the barrier. Hermod found his way to the hall where Hel had her dwelling. There the goddess presided over a silent feast, with Balder and Nanna seated in a place of honor.

Hermod was a plain-spoken warrior, not a poet, but his account of Asgard's weeping gods and desolate palaces must have moved the Queen of Death. She proposed a test. If every creature and object in all the worlds wept openly for Balder, she would accept that torrent of tears as a ransom, and send their loved one back to his homeland. But if anything, or anyone, stayed dry-eyed, she would keep Balder captive in her court forever.

Hermod returned to Asgard and conveyed the challenge. Messengers were quick to carry the word to every creature and sphere of existence. Just as everything in the cosmos had promised to keep Balder from harm, so they now agreed, each in their separate ways, to weep him home from Hel. Humans sobbed, hounds howled, a crystal drop fell from the hawk's unwinking eye, stones released waters hidden in their depths. The universe vibrated with ululations, and the tears of all creation soaked through the earth and nearly flooded Hel.

Yet the ransom was not complete, the messengers discovered. On the way back to Asgard, they stopped to rest in a cave, taking shelter, perhaps, from the sky's own weeping. There they met a giantess whose eyes were dry and empty. They asked her to join in the lamentation. She replied: "Balder was no use to me alive or dead. Let Hel hold what she has."

So Balder remained in Hel's household, and the gods raged. Later they discovered that the giantess had been Loki in yet another disguise.

Odin brooded. He recalled the witch's prophecy at the time of Balder's dreams.

She had spoken obscurely—of murder to come, of its yet unborn avenger, of the mortal princess who would carry Odin's seed in her womb. Only with Balder's death had the riddlings come clear. Now, after all that had passed, Odin understood. To punish the killer of one son, he would have to beget another, born for this purpose alone, from a woman named by the seer—Rinda, the daughter of a King among the Rus.

Odin chose a disguise for himself. He became a young soldier, with muscles that rippled and weapons that gleamed, in hopes that such accouterments would captivate a maiden who had reached an age of longings and daydreams.

When this visitor arrived at the hall of Rinda's father, he was welcomed with all the courtesies owed to a valiant stranger. Platters of steaming meat were served to him, and thralls refilled his drinking horn as soon as the last drop had left it. Poets regaled the company with tales of old victories and new ones.

While his hosts enjoyed a rhymed account of their favorite battles, Odin slipped off to meet the Princess in a dark corner. But he found that Rinda did not share her father's hospitable nature. This was not the pliable green girl of his expectations. She dismissed his wooing, and when, fueled by more mead, he returned for a second sally on her virtue, she scorched his ears with curses.

Greater magic was needed. Odin left the hall and strode into the surrounding forest. He stripped a sheet of bark from a birch tree and inscribed upon it several rows of magic symbols. Then he returned to the hall, stepping over heaps of drunken sleepers, to find Rinda crouched near the hearth, sucking the marrow from a mutton bone. As if in jest, he struck her with the bark.

Rinda dropped the bone, reared up, opened her mouth and roared like a she-bear. She ran through the hall in a frenzy, overturning benches, flinging knives, striking anyone who stood in her path. Odin lingered in the doorway while she strangled a hapless slave. Then he wandered off into the woods, leaving his host to deal with the crisis.

By the next morning, all was quiet. The Princess had been overpowered by the combined efforts of a dozen of the King's mightiest warriors and locked into a small chamber at the far end of the hall. Odin, who had gone away to don the face and form of an old herb-woman, returned to present himself to Rinda's distraught father. The crone spoke soothing words and held up a basket of tangled roots and pungent grasses, promising to effect a rapid cure. The King said that he would gladly let the woman treat the girl, but he feared for the safety of anyone who approached her. Even now, her shouts, thumps, howls and curses reverberated throughout the hall.

The crone laughed. She had dealt with worse cases, she said, and asked only to be left alone with the patient. At their lord's behest, a pair of thralls pulled away the timbers and stones that had been piled up

*A master of disguises, Odin often journeyed undetected
through the realms of giants, dwarfs and humankind.*

against the door as a barricade. Then they scuttled back, eager to be well out of the way. The old woman drew the huge bolts, turned keys in locks and opened the door just wide enough to slip inside, commanding them to seal the room again behind her.

For a while the household heard only roaring. Slowly it died away to silence. Many hours later, the old woman called through the door. Servants once again removed the barricades, and the crone emerged. Behind her, curled up in a corner, Rinda slept. Her breathing was tranquil and her expression untroubled. All would be well now, the healer promised. She brushed aside the King's proffered payment and disappeared.

When the Princess woke, she babbled an incoherent tale. A woman had come to her, shifted shape into a god, and taken her by force. The house dismissed this delusion as a vestige of her madness, until her belly swelled. She bore a boy of exceptional size and strength. His tiny fists clenched and flexed, as if in search of a sword to wield or an arrow to shoot.

Odin, far away now, smiled at the news. The prophecy would be fulfilled: Rinda's child would grow to slay Balder's killer. But Odin was never satisfied. He lusted after perfect knowledge of the future, as if omniscience could bring omnipotence in its train. He was to learn, in time, that this was folly.

His quest for wisdom took him deep into the land of Hel, where souls slept under long cairns of heaped-up stones. He went up to one of these barrows and uttered a summoning spell. Out of the mound's depths came a wail. The spirit was reluctant to be roused. Yet it was bound by his magic and came forth.

Odin's eyes widened. He had known he was calling up the ghost of a witch, but only when the specter rose did he see it was Heid, reborn from the Vanir sorceress, Gullveig, who had been tortured in Asgard so long ago.

Grim words poured from her twisted mouth. First, she spoke of past events, her tongue a spade that turned over the earth of buried times, exposing worms and secrets. Then, when she had thus proved the clarity of her sight, the Sibyl began to look forward.

One after another, terrible visions unfolded: the goddess Frigg weeping over the woes of Asgard; Loki trussed up beside a sulfurous spring; a sunless shore where dead men waded through poisoned waters; a great dragon sucking the blood from their bodies and leaving their flesh and bones as carrion for the Fenris wolf, monstrous spawn of Loki.

The Sibyl paused, fixed Odin with her eyes, and asked him, "Would you know more?" He pressed her to continue.

She foresaw the armies of slain warriors storming out of Valholl; the world shuddering in universal warfare, as sons of the same mothers turned upon one another and shed their common blood. She told how the great ash tree at the world's center would shake, and the serpent that girdled the earth thrash in fury; how Loki

*The warnings of the Sibyl echoed in the
firmament: The gods' own evil would redound
upon them, and they were doomed.*

would sail from the north on a ship of doom, bringing the armies of darkness.

"Would you know more?"

All this she foretold to Odin: A troop of demons slaughtering the gods with swords of fire; mountains toppling, stars plummeting, the sun turning black; Asgard's palaces awash with blood; Odin himself mauled to death by the Fenris wolf; the earth drowning in an ocean; the whine of the winds, then silence.

"Would you know more?"

There was nothing more to know. The Sibyl's ghost sank once more into the grave among the rocks.

Such was the arrogance of Odin that, despite these warnings, he believed he could deflect destiny. The seeress had spoken of troops pouring forth from Valholl for universal warfare. He resolved to stock his fortress with a fighting force that could withstand any number of enemy onslaughts. To form this garrison, he would recruit the boldest and bravest warriors he could find. He had always welcomed earth's most valiant heroes to his household. Those who had fallen were received as honored guests in his hall from the moment their souls were wrenched from their bodies by an enemy spear or arrow-thrust.

But Odin knew well the might of his foes in the conflict to come. He would have to muster men in far greater numbers. If necessary, he would snatch the boldest human heroes from the land of the living before their fated time.

It was a simple matter for Odin, the divine magician, to intervene in the outcome of a battle and effect the death of those who had been meant to survive it. So Odin became a thief of souls.

To help him gather up these troops, he summoned the Valkyries—goddesses of carnage, haunters of corpse-strewn battlefields. Their names expressed their natures: One was called Shrieking, another Screaming, a third Raging.

Like that other divine sisterhood, the Norns, Valkyries were adept at the womanly skills of weaving, but their machine was the loom of slaughter. It had human heads for weights and blood-slicked spears for heddle-rods. The web of war they made on it was a mesh of human gore and entrails. Odin commanded them to watch as worldlings fought, and choose the candidates for his armies.

The Valkyries then carried the souls of the battle-slain to Valholl. There Odin received them in a golden hall, roofed with shields and raftered with spears. Each day, his ghostly guests enjoyed war games, duels and wrestling matches in the spacious courtyards. Each night they came together to feast and trade tales of valor. Their meat was the flesh of a sacred boar that was butchered each night but rose up miraculously each morning, to fatten all day and be slaughtered and cooked anew. Its savor, so the talespinners said, was sweeter than that of any such beast reared by human husbandry. Indulging in the pleasures of comradeship and combat, the company was content, but always battle-ready.

The Valkyries scoured earth's battlefields to claim
the souls of dying heroes. These champions were borne
to Asgard to constitute Odin's ghostly army.

Confident that Asgard's forces would now win even the worst of wars, Odin and his fellow gods immersed themselves in a round of routs and revels, culminating in a great banquet hosted by the sea-god, Aegir. Everyone came willingly, for the lord of the waters was a famous brewer of ale.

As the drink flowed freely, the gods grew sentimental. They began to treat one another with exaggerated courtesy, lavishing compliments on the food, the company and the service of the feast. One attendant in particular was singled out for praise: How generously he replenished the platters and drinking horns; how assiduously he encouraged the guests to eat their fill; how swiftly he responded to requests of any kind.

Loki, who was among the company, could stand no more. Some accounts claimed he was jealous of praise heaped on any but himself; others that he was sickened by these honeyed words and by the smirk of the servant who received them. He pulled his knife from a joint of venison and hurled it. The waiter died before the grin had left his face.

The gods were outraged. Violence at a feast broke all laws of hospitality. They hounded Loki from the hall. The body of the slave was dragged away and fresh straw scattered to soak up his blood. Then a roasted ox came smoking from the spit, and the diners turned their attention to their trenchers once again.

Loki wandered off and sulked in the woods for a few hours before bursting in upon the company once more. At the sight of him the Aesir abandoned a drinking song mid-chorus. In the silence, Loki scanned the upturned faces. He called out to Odin, reminding him of the days when they had been sworn friends and blood brothers, and how the chief of the gods would never drink ale unless his good companion Loki was there by his side.

Then, one by one, Loki addressed the other gods and goddesses, reminding them of past sins and scandals, dredging up secrets they would have preferred to keep well buried. As he spoke, he pointed his finger at one victim after another. This one, he said, was a whore who cuckolded her spouse with lovers of both sexes; that one sitting by her side was a liar, a coward and a cheat.

Up and down both sides of the hall he went, and few were spared. Loki promised them all a dose of gall to flavor their drinks, and he succeeded. The gods tried to counterattack with a torrent of abuse, but Loki deflected every gibe and insult.

When he had exhausted his memory, Loki stunned the Aesir with a parting shot. He announced that his had been the guiding hand when Hoder threw the mistletoe at Balder. His had been the eye that stayed dry when all the world sought to weep Balder home from Hel.

As he spoke, Loki edged toward the door, but before he took his leave, he declared that his son, the Fenris wolf, would soon break its chains, heralding the destruction of the gods. Then he vanished.

For a moment, there was silence in the hall. Suddenly, benches were flung away, tables overturned, knives and trenchers thrown and scattered. The gods of Asgard rose as one and rushed after Loki, borne on a tide of shame and rage.

Slipping from one shape to another, Loki outran his pursuers. He fled far from the palaces of Asgard, over the broad plains, along the coast's rocky inlets, up into the forested mountains where all the streams and rivers of the north were born. There on the high slopes, he found a hiding-place. The house he chose had a door in each of its four walls, allowing Loki to keep a lookout in all directions.

Here he stayed, protected by his own magic. Each day he assumed the form of a salmon, the king of fishes, and lurked beneath the waterfall. And every night, he resumed his usual shape. Loki's sojourn under the waters inspired him to devise a new way of catching fish: He was the first to make a fishing net.

One evening, as he worked by the hearth, perfecting the knots of this invention, he heard voices. The Aesir were approaching. He flung his net into the fire, slipped back into the form of a fish and hid in the stream.

When the Aesir stormed in, the hut was empty. But the burning net had left its pattern in the ashes of the hearth. The gods knew at once that this was a device for trapping slippery creatures. They succeeded in fashioning another like it. A test for its powers was close at hand: Outside the hut, a large salmon leaped in the stream. Thor caught it, and as the great fish thrashed and struggled in the snare, he saw that it was Loki.

By the weight of their will, the gods forced Loki to resume his old shape, and decided upon a punishment suited to the horror of his crimes. They dragged him to a cave in the maw of the earth. Next to a foul-smelling spring, they bound his body over the edges of three sharp rocks. For fetters, they used no ordinary metal, but the twisted and knotted entrails of Narfi, one of Loki's own sons.

Then the gods hung a poisonous serpent on a branch over their supine captive, placed so that its venom would fall on his face. There they left him to languish. But Loki was permitted one small comfort in his underground prison: His wife, the goddess Sigyn, came to sit by his side. She held a cup to catch the dripping poison. Whenever the vessel filled up, Sigyn was forced to turn away and empty it. Then the acid fell directly onto Loki's skin, hissing and burning. So great was Loki's agony that his writhings made the whole earth quake.

Odin came to stand in triumph over the prisoner, to watch him straining and screaming in his bonds. Then he remembered the words of the Sibyl in the underworld. Just as she had foretold, Loki now lay in chains beside a sulfurous spring. And many of the things that had seemed strange when she spoke now made sense. Odin realized that everything she had prophesied would come to pass. The doom of the gods could not be averted. The world's end was near. In the distance, he heard the howling of a wolf.

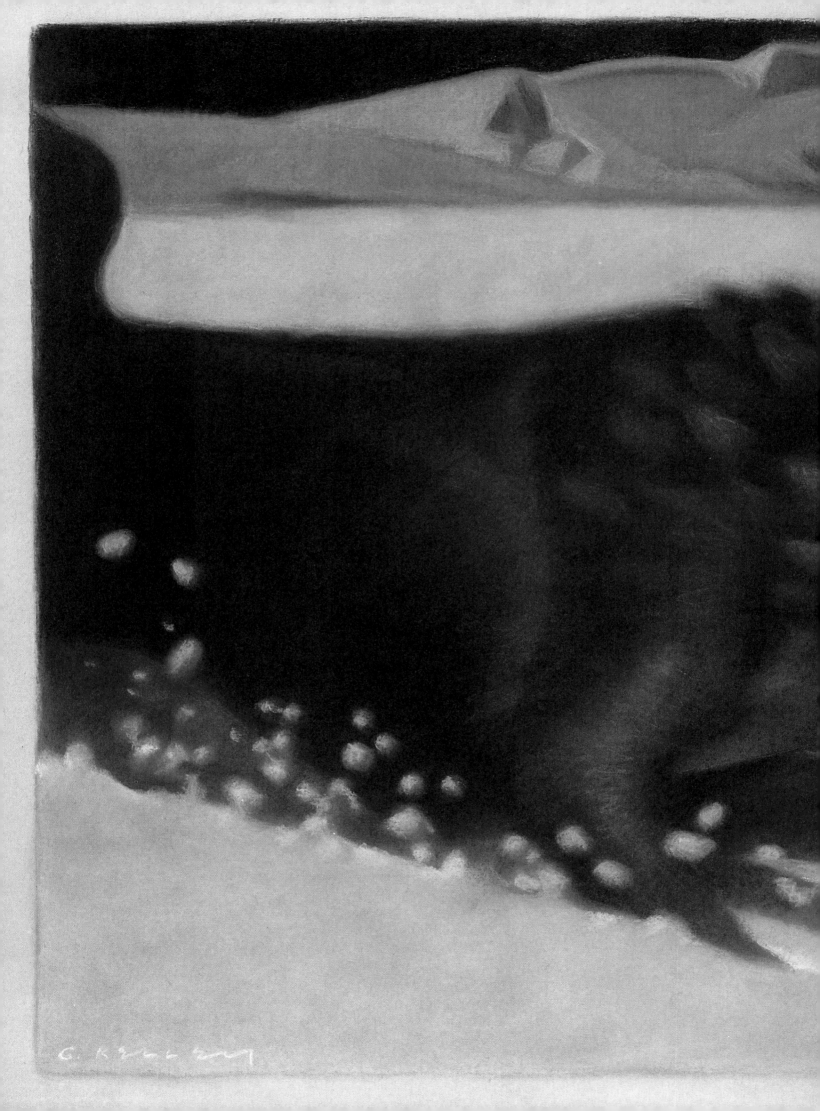

Doom Unleashed

No matter how passionately the gods of the north craved eternal life and parried threats to their dominion, they knew that a great cataclysm would someday overtake them. At time's beginning, the three Norns—female weavers of fate, immortals themselves, more powerful than the greatest of gods—had foretold the ultimate destruction of the cosmos. Sibyls and witches had taught the omens of the coming catastrophe. The road to doom thus was all too clear.

First, the world turned cold and dark. For three years of unbroken night, one terrible winter followed another, with frosts hard as iron. Birds fell dead from the sky, trees perished, and the seas were armored in ice.

Deep in the earth, the monstrous Fenris wolf struggled in the chains that the gods had forged, formed of wonders and impossibilities: the cry of a cat, the beard of a woman, a mountain's roots, the tendons of a bear, the breath of a fish and spittle blown from the beak of a flying bird. Confined in these bonds the wolf might be, but its whelps escaped from their subterranean lair and roamed freely across the world. Nourished on all humankind's evil, the cubs grew massive beyond imagining, until they were able to leap up and snatch the sun in their jaws. At the moment their fangs tore the golden disk, the wolf burst its bonds. Fire spurted from its eyes and nostrils; blood dripped from its maw. Erupting out of the earth, the monster charged across the frozen plains, igniting the trees with its breath. The flames could be seen from the towers of Asgard, heralding that holocaust known as Ragnarök, the Twilight of the Gods.

Vengeful and blood-hungry, the Fenris wolf erupted from the underworld pit where the gods had chained it. Its liberation signaled that the end of the world was imminent.

Once the Fenris wolf was loose, horror followed upon horror. All the evil creatures of the world emerged from their lairs: dragons coated with slime and breathing sulfurous fumes, snakes dripping venom from forked tongues, rats with eyes of fire, hosts of flies and stinging insects, parasites that burrowed into tender flesh. The earth quaked and the ocean savaged the coasts. The Midgard serpent, which had lurked on the sea bed since the morning of creation, surfaced and headed for land, its jaws yawning and fangs gleaming, spitting jets of poison that rose in an arc to scorch the vault of heaven.

Meanwhile, the giants, who had nursed grudges against the gods for eons, rose up in wrath. They remembered how they had been cozened, mocked and cheated, how their treasures had been stolen and their women seduced, how their strength had been exploited and their labors unrewarded.

Even as they marched from their land of Jötunheim to Asgard, Yggdrasil, the great ash tree at the world's center, cracked open, terrifying the sacred creatures that dwelled in its foliage: a golden cockerel, a squirrel, a goat, four stags, a snake and a falcon.

The quivering of Yggdrasil's leaves raised a terrible wind in Asgard. Heimdall, the sentry of the gods, heard its wailing from his post at the walls of Asgard, where the bridge of rainbows spanned the worlds, and saw the giants on the march. The watchman blew a great blast on his horn to summon the divinities to a council of war. They came from their palaces, armed and ready. The prophecies were known to them. A sorceress had foretold this moment with the words: "An ax age, a sword age; shields will be cloven; a wind age, a wolf age." Nothing in heaven or earth, not even the gods themselves, was free from fear.

Omens of catastrophe appeared in every sphere. The great ash tree at the core of the universe cracked asunder, and Heimdall, the heavenly sentinel, blew a warning blast on his horn.

When Heimdall's horn sounded its warning, Odin, greatest of the gods, made his way through the groves of winter-blasted oaks to a shrine concealed in a secret place, protected against intruders by invisible barricades constructed of spells and curses. He went to seek counsel from Mimir, who had once been a god of wisdom and prophecy.

Mimir was not among the living. He had been killed in a feud long before. But Odin had preserved his mentor's head, intact and uncorrupted, by means of charms and sorcery, and though Mimir no longer had the breath of life, he retained—through Odin's occult skills—the power of thought and speech. Now, for the last time, Odin descended to the head's holy resting place. The poets did not reveal the advice offered to the All-Father. It may have been that Mimir's lips gave voice to the dread in Odin's heart—that nothing could be done to change the outcome of the war. Yet it must be fought. With this knowledge, Odin returned to his fortress, Valholl, carrying the spear that was a symbol of kingship, and leading his animal familiars, two wolves and a pair of sacred ravens. The creatures were restless, for they smelled blood.

Odin gathered the other gods and goddesses about him and told them to prepare for the final battle. The strategies they planned, and the orders they were given, were not recorded by the chroniclers, but it was certain that magic would play as great a part in the confrontation as arrows, shields, axes and the thunderbolts of Thor.

The walls of the fortress shook with a rumbling that its denizens knew for the sound of the enemy battalions coming closer. The deities of Asgard watched and waited. The time for words was past.

Questing for help in a time of terror, Odin sought wisdom greater than his own. He consulted the magically preserved head of a long-departed sage to learn what actions might forestall disaster.

From all directions, by land and sea, the enemies of the gods advanced on Asgard. In the south appeared the troops of Surt, demon lord of the fire giants, whose sword glowed like a memory of the vanished sun. At every pace, steam hissed through fissures in the earth, and each of his footsteps left a print of flame on the ground. His army was shielded by a ring of fire.

Out of the howling tempest, dreadful shapes skimmed over the sea. From the west came a ship crewed by phantoms and captained by the giant, Hrym. But more terrible by far was the vessel sailing from the north, bearing the banner of Loki, evil incarnate.

For a long time he had languished underground near a spring of poisoned water, bound by the gods with ropes made from the entrails of one of his own offspring, tied to rocks and exposed to the acid venom that oozed from a serpent's jaws. But now he had broken free from his place of torment and rode into battle to avenge himself on those who had confined him there.

The ship on which Loki sailed, known as *Naglfar*, was the most sinister of vessels. Since earliest times, the ships of the north had been hewn from oak trees, but this craft was built from the fingernails of dead men. For many generations, wizards presiding over funeral rites had insisted that the nails of corpses be cut to the very quick in order to thwart the evil shipwrights of the underworld; for they knew the prophecies concerning Ragnarök and the role that a ship of nails would play in it.

Yet despite all their efforts, the construction and launching of *Naglfar* could only be postponed; it could not be forfended. Now the vessel approached the shore, bearing its ghastly blue-skinned crew mustered from the dead in Hel's frozen wastes.

A flotilla of unearthly enemies sailed against the gods. Its flagship was a vessel made of dead mens' fingernails, and Loki, lord of destruction, stood at its helm.

The field of conflict was the square plain called Vigridr, which stretched out before Valholl and measured, said the bards, a thousand leagues on every side. As the giants advanced on foot and on horseback, the sky cracked open and Bifrost, the rainbow bridge that linked Asgard to the earth, burst into flames and crumbled.

The gods were led into battle by Odin, who wore a coat of mail and a golden helmet plumed with eagle's wings. He made straight for the Fenris wolf, but his strength could not avail against this worst of monsters. The wolf opened its huge jaws, engulfed the father of the gods, and devoured him.

Those of his troops who witnessed Odin's sudden and ignominious death were transfixed with horror, and became easy prey for the swinging battle-axes of the giants. Odin's downfall was unseen by Thor, the god of thunder, who was grappling with the Midgard serpent. His thunderbolts glanced off the creature's scales with no visible effect. Then Thor raised his hammer and, expending his last strength, shattered the wedge-shaped head. The serpent had its revenge with its dying breath: It exhaled a cloud of venomous smoke that sent Thor choking down to Hel. Loki stood in the midst of the gory field, seeking an opponent worthy of his might. His eyes lit on Heimdall, and recalling old, still-rankling resentments, he charged at the watchman, wielding a sword and a knife as tapered as an icicle. The two were well matched in war skills, and neither could be bested, but finally their weapons struck home, and Asgard's sentinel and Asgard's bane fell upon the earth together. None were left to mourn, for all the golden gods and goddesses of Asgard were dead.

In the final battle, on the great plain before Asgard, Thor wrestled with the monstrous Midgard serpent, matching his thunderbolts and hammer against the reptile's venomous exhalations.

With Thor no longer present
to preserve the order of the universe, animal
and human, giant, dwarf and spirit were enveloped in chaos. Large creatures devoured
small ones, men and women set upon one another, betrayed their kin, smothered their
own children, tore the flesh and broke the
bones of their neighbors. Armies rebelled
against their commanders, sailors mutinied at
sea. Thralls died of starvation on the verges
of fallow fields, and the wild beasts of the forests turned and pursued their hunters. Soon
all the species of the several worlds had disappeared. Only a few birds of prey swooped
down from otherworldly eyries to claim such
carrion as they could find.

Winds wailed through the abandoned halls
of gods and giants alike, bearing upon their
currents the reek of blood. The earth itself
began to lose its form, and the stars fell like
exhausted swallows dropping into the sea
after too long a flight.

The three realms of Asgard, Midgard and
Jötunheim ignited. Some bards said the fire
giant Surt had perpetrated this act with his
dying breath. The glare of destruction illumined the skies as once the sun and moon
had done, but not a single living thing was
alive to witness the sight.

The spear-raftered halls of Valholl and the
palaces of the gods were consumed in the
conflagration. Not a tree remained upright in
the sacred groves, not a runestone was left
standing. Only scorched soil and baked mud
remained, scarred and furrowed by fissures.

Then the seas and rivers rose and ruptured
their banks. Cliffs crumbled, mountains sank
in upon themselves. Enormous waves swept
everything before them, and waters cooled
and covered the ravaged earth. But the heavens continued to burn for eons after. This
was the way the old world ended.

*The aftermath of war was emptiness—all
giants, gods and humans dead. Only those
birds that fed on corpses' flesh survived, and
even they disappeared in the great fires and
floods that engulfed the earth.*

By means unknown to prophets or poets, a new world emerged out of the wreckage of what had been before. Rising slowly from the floodwaters, this virgin earth was green and fertile. A daughter of the old sun, more luminous and life-giving than her parent had been, appeared in the heavens and shone down upon an age of hope.

Rivers began to flow once more, springs bubbled up, brooks raced down the newly risen mountainsides where young birds nested and saplings grew. Once more salmon leaped in the streams, and deer browsed among the tender shoots on the woodland floor.

Miraculously, two human beings, one male and one female, had survived the devastation. They were the progenitors of a new race that would in time repopulate the earth. Yet they did not dwell alone.

Gods also ventured once again into this brave new world. Balder, the most beautiful and virtuous of the old divinities, who had been murdered by Loki's machinations, returned to life and took over the task of protecting humankind. With him came other deities—sons of Thor and sons of Odin—to dwell once more in the heavens and remember the times that had passed.

Amid the meadows of this peacable kingdom stood Gimlé, the home of good and righteous folk. It had a roof of golden thatch and halls built of red gold. When its inhabitants walked abroad in the fresh and fragrant air, they trod upon strange objects in the grass: stones carved with runes, amulets of inexplicable purpose, and golden chess pieces from the games of the vanished gods.

Yet all was not, nor could be, perfection in this terrestrial paradise. Under the earth lurked a dragon, newborn or resurrected, biding its time. When it would strike, no poet, sage or sibyl could say.

A new world, green and fertile, rose from the mud and ashes of the old. Birds, beasts and humans reappeared to dwell once more upon the land. But underground a dragon—evil incarnate—waited.

Picture Credits

The sources for the illustrations in this book are shown below. When it is known, the name of the artist precedes the source of the picture.

Cover: Artwork by John Howe. 1-5: Artwork by Jennifer Eachus. 6-29: Artwork by Stuart Robertson. 30-31: Artwork by Tim Pearce. 33: Artwork by Anita Kunz. 36-41: Artwork by Nick Harris. 42: Artwork by Martin Knowelden. 45: Artwork by Jennifer Eachus. 46-47: Artwork by Nick Harris. 48-51: Artwork by Yvonne Gilbert. 52-55: Artwork by Kevin Grey. 57: Artwork by Nick Harris. 58-59: Artwork by Tim Pearce. 60-61: Artwork by Nick Harris. 62-69: Artwork by John Howe. 70-71: Artwork by George Sharp. 72-73: Border artwork by Philip Argent. 74-79: By courtesy of the Board of Trustees of the Victoria and Albert Museum. 78-81: Border artwork by Philip Argent. 82: Artwork by Colin Stimpson. 83: Border artwork by Philip Argent. 85: Artwork by Tess Stone. 86-87: Border artwork by Philip Argent. 88-89: By courtesy of the Board of Trustees of the Victoria and Albert Museum. 90-99: Artwork by Kinuko Y. Craft. 100-123: Arthur Rackham, from *The Rhinegold and the Valkyrie* (1910) and *The Twilight of the Gods* (1911), William Heinemann, by permission of Barbara Edwards. 100-125: Artwork based on a border illustration by Charles Robinson, 1898. 126-139: Artwork by Gary Kelley. 144: Artwork by Jennifer Eachus.

Bibliography

Abrahams, Ethel B., *Greek Dress*. London: John Murray, 1908.

Aldington, Richard, and Delano Ames, transl., *New Larousse Encyclopedia of Mythology*. London: The Hamlyn Publishing Group, 1985.*

Allegro, John, *The Lost Gods*. London: Michael Joseph, 1977.

Anesaki, Masaharu, *The Mythology of All Races: Japanese*. Vol. 8. Boston: Marshall Jones Company, 1928.*

Bhattacharji, Sukumari, *The Indian Theogony*. Cambridge: Cambridge University Press, 1970.

Bonnard, André, *Greek Civilization*. Transl. by A. Lytton Sells. London: George Allen & Unwin, 1962.

Browning, Robert, ed., *The Greek World*. London: Thames and Hudson, 1985.

Campbell, Joseph, *The Masks of God: Oriental Mythology*. London: Secker & Warburg, 1962.

Carnoy, Albert J., and A. Berridale Keith, *The Mythology of All Races: Indian, Iranian*. Vol. 5. Boston: Marshall Jones Company, 1917.

Cavendish, Richard, ed., *Man, Myth and Magic*. 11 vols. New York: Marshall Cavendish, 1983.

Dasent, Sir George Webbe, *Popular Tales from the Norse*. Edinburgh: David Douglas, 1933.

Davidson, H. R. Ellis, *Gods and Myths of Northern Europe*. Harmondsworth, England: Penguin Books, 1964.*

Davis, F. Hadland, *Myths and Legends of Japan*. London: George Harrap, 1919.

Dumezil, Georges, *Loki*. Paris: Editions G.P. Maisonneuve, 1948.

Eliade, Mircea, *Patterns in Comparative Religion*. Transl. by Rosemary Sheed. London: Sheed & Ward, 1958.*

Erman, Adolf, *Life in Ancient Egypt*. Transl. by H. M. Tirard. London: Macmillan, 1894.*

Faulkner, Raymond O., transl., and Carol Andrews, ed., *The Ancient Egyptian Book of the Dead*. London: British Museum Publications, 1985.*

Foote, P.G., and D.M. Wilson, *The Viking Achievement*. London: Sidgwick & Jackson, 1980.*

Gayley, Charles Mills, *The Classic Myths*. Boston: Ginn and Company, 1911.

Graves, Robert, *The Greek Myths*. Vols. 1 and 2. Harmondsworth, England: Penguin Books, 1985.

Harshananda, Swami, *Hindu Gods and Goddesses*. Mysore, India: Sri Ramakrishna Ashrama, 1982.

Hesiod, *The Works of Hesiod, Callimachus and Theogius*. Transl. by the Rev. J. Banks. London: Henry G. Bohn, 1856.

Homer:
The Homeric Hymns. Transl. by Andrew Lang. London: George Allen, 1899.*
The Odyssey. Transl. by E.V. Rieu. Harmondsworth, England: Penguin Books, 1967.*
The Iliad. Transl. by E.V. Rieu. Harmondsworth, England: Penguin Books, 1986.*

Ions, Veronica:
Egyptian Mythology. Twickenham, England: Newnes Books, 1986.*
Indian Mythology. Twickenham, England: Newnes Books, 1986.*

James, E.O., *The Cult of the Mother-Goddess*. London: Thames and Hudson, 1959.

James, T.G.H., *Pharaoh's People*. Oxford: Oxford University Press, 1985.*

Leach, Maria, ed., *Funk & Wagnall's Standard Dictionary of Folklore, Mythology and Legend*. San Francisco: Harper & Row, 1984.*

Mackenzie, Donald A.:
Indian Myth and Legend. London: Gresham Publishing, 1913.
Teutonic Myth and Legend. London: Gresham Publishing, 1934.

MacCulloch, J.A.:
The Celtic and Scandinavian Religions. New York: Hutchinson's University Library, 1948.*
The Mythology of All Races: Eddic. Vol. 2. Boston: Marshall Jones Company, 1930.*
Religion of the Ancient Celts. Edinburgh: T. & T. Clark, 1911.

Macfie, J.M., *Myths and Legends of India*. Edinburgh: T. & T. Clark, 1924.

Magnusson, Magnus, *Hammer of the North*. London: Orbis Publishing, 1976.*

Michalowski, Kazimierz, *The Art of Ancient Egypt*. London: Thames and Hudson, 1969.

Muller, Max, and Sir James George Scott, *The Mythology of All Races: Egyptian, Indo-Chinese*. Vol. 12. Boston: Marshall Jones Company, 1918.

Narayan, R.K., *Gods, Demons and Others*. London: Heinemann, 1965.*

The Sister Nivedia (Margaret E. Noble); *Cradle Tales of Hinduism*. New York: Longmans, Green and Company, 1907.

O'Flaherty, Wendy Doniger, *Asceticism and Eroticism in the Mythology of Siva*. London: Oxford University Press, 1973.

Otto, Eberhard, *Egyptian Art and the Culture of Osiris and Amon*. London: Thames and Hudson, 1968.

Ovid, *The Metamorphoses*. Transl. by Mary M. Innes. Harmondsworth, England: Penguin Books, 1968.*

Piggott, Juliet, *Japanese Mythology*. Feltham, England: Newnes Books, 1984.*

Saxo Grammaticus, *The History of the Danes*. Vols. 1 and 2. Transl. by Peter Fisher, ed. by Hilda Ellis Davidson. Cambridge: D.S. Brewer, and Totowa, New Jersey: Rowman and Littlefield, 1979.*

Smith, William Stevenson, *Ancient Egypt*. Boston: Museum of Fine Arts, 1960.

Stead, Miriam, *Egyptian Life*. London: British Museum Publications, 1986.

Sturluson, Snorri, *The Prose Edda*. Transl. by Jean Young. Berkeley: University of California Press, 1964.*

Tannahill, Reay, *Food in History*. London: Eyre Methuen, 1973.

Taylor, Paul B., and W.H. Auden, transl., *The Elder Edda*. London: Faber & Faber, 1969.*

Thompson, Stith, *Motif Index of Folk Literature*. Bloomington: Indiana University Press, 1955.

Turville-Petre, E.O.G., *Myth and Religion of the North*. London: Weidenfeld and Nicolson, 1964.*

Walker, Barbara G., *The Women's Encyclopedia of Myths and Secrets*. San Francisco: Harper & Row, 1983.

Walker, Benjamin, *Hindu World*. Vols. 1 and 2. London: George Allen & Unwin, 1968.

Zimmer, Heinrich, *Myths and Symbols in Indian Art and Civilization*. Ed. by Joseph Campbell. New York: Pantheon Books, 1947.

Titles marked with an asterisk were especially helpful in the preparation of this volume.

Acknowledgments

The editors wish to thank the following persons and institutions for their help in the preparation of this volume: Guy Andrews, London; M. Ayres, London; Charles Boyle, London; Lesley Coleman, London; Dipali Ghosh, The British Library, London; Fred Grunfeld, Mallorca, Spain; The London Library; J.P. Losty, India Office Library, London; Robin Olson, London; Victoria and Albert Museum, London.

Time-Life Books Inc.
is a wholly owned subsidiary of

TIME INCORPORATED

FOUNDER: Henry R. Luce 1898-1967

Editor-in-Chief: Henry Anatole Grunwald
Chairman and Chief Executive Officer: J. Richard Munro
President and Chief Operating Officer: N. J. Nicholas Jr.
Chairman of the Executive Committee: Ralph P. Davidson
Corporate Editor: Ray Cave
Group Vice President, Books: Reginald K. Brack Jr.
Vice President, Books: George Artandi

TIME-LIFE BOOKS INC.

EDITOR: George Constable
Director of Design: Louis Klein
Director of Editorial Resources: Phyllis K. Wise
Acting Text Director: Ellen Phillips
Editorial Board: Russell B. Adams Jr., Dale M. Brown, Roberta Conlan, Thomas H. Flaherty, Donia Ann Steele, Rosalind Stubenberg, Kit van Tulleken, Henry Woodhead
Director of Photography and Research: John Conrad Weiser

EUROPEAN EDITOR: Kit van Tulleken
Assistant European Editor: Gillian Moore
Design Director: Ed Skyner
Chief of Research: Vanessa Kramer
Chief Sub-Editor: Ilse Gray .

PRESIDENT: Christopher T. Linen
Executive Vice President: John M. Fahey Jr.
Senior Vice Presidents: James L. Mercer, Leopoldo Toralballa
Vice Presidents: Stephen L. Bair, Ralph J. Cuomo, Terence J. Furlong, Neal Goff, Stephen L. Goldstein, Juanita T. James, Hallett Johnson III, Robert H. Smith, Paul R. Stewart
Director of Production Services: Robert J. Passantino

THE ENCHANTED WORLD

SERIES DIRECTOR: Ellen Galford
Picture Editor: Mark Karras
Designer: Mary Staples
Series Secretary: Eugénie Romer

Editorial Staff for *Gods and Goddesses*
Writer/Researcher: Ellen Dupont
Design Assistant: Julie Busby
Sub-Editor: Jane Hawker

Editorial Production
Coordinator: Maureen Kelly
Production Assistant: Deborah Fulham
Editorial Department: Theresa John, Debra Lelliott

Correspondents: Elisabeth Kraemer-Singh (Bonn); Dorothy Bacon (London); Maria Vincenza Aloisi (Paris); Ann Natanson (Rome).

Chief Series Consultant

Tristram Potter Coffin, Professor of English at the University of Pennsylvania, is a leading authority on folklore. He is the author or editor of numerous books and more than one hundred articles. His best-known works are *The British Traditional Ballad in North America, The Old Ball Game, The Book of Christmas Folklore* and *The Female Hero.*

This volume is one of a series that is based on myths, legends and folk tales.

Other Publications:

SUCCESSFUL PARENTING
HEALTHY HOME COOKING
UNDERSTANDING COMPUTERS
YOUR HOME
THE KODAK LIBRARY OF CREATIVE PHOTOGRAPHY
GREAT MEALS IN MINUTES
THE CIVIL WAR
PLANET EARTH
COLLECTOR'S LIBRARY OF THE CIVIL WAR
THE EPIC OF FLIGHT
THE GOOD COOK
WORLD WAR II
HOME REPAIR AND IMPROVEMENT
THE OLD WEST

For information on and a full description of any of the Time-Life Books series listed above, please write:
Reader Information
Time-Life Books
541 North Fairbanks Court
Chicago, Illinois 60611

Library of Congress Cataloguing in Publication Data
Gods and Goddesses.
    (The Enchanted world)
    Bibliography: p.
    1. Creation. 2. Mythology.
I. Time-Life Books   II. Series
BL226.G62 1987   291.2'11   86-30170

ISBN 0-8094-5273-1
ISBN 0-8094-5274-X (lib. bdg.)

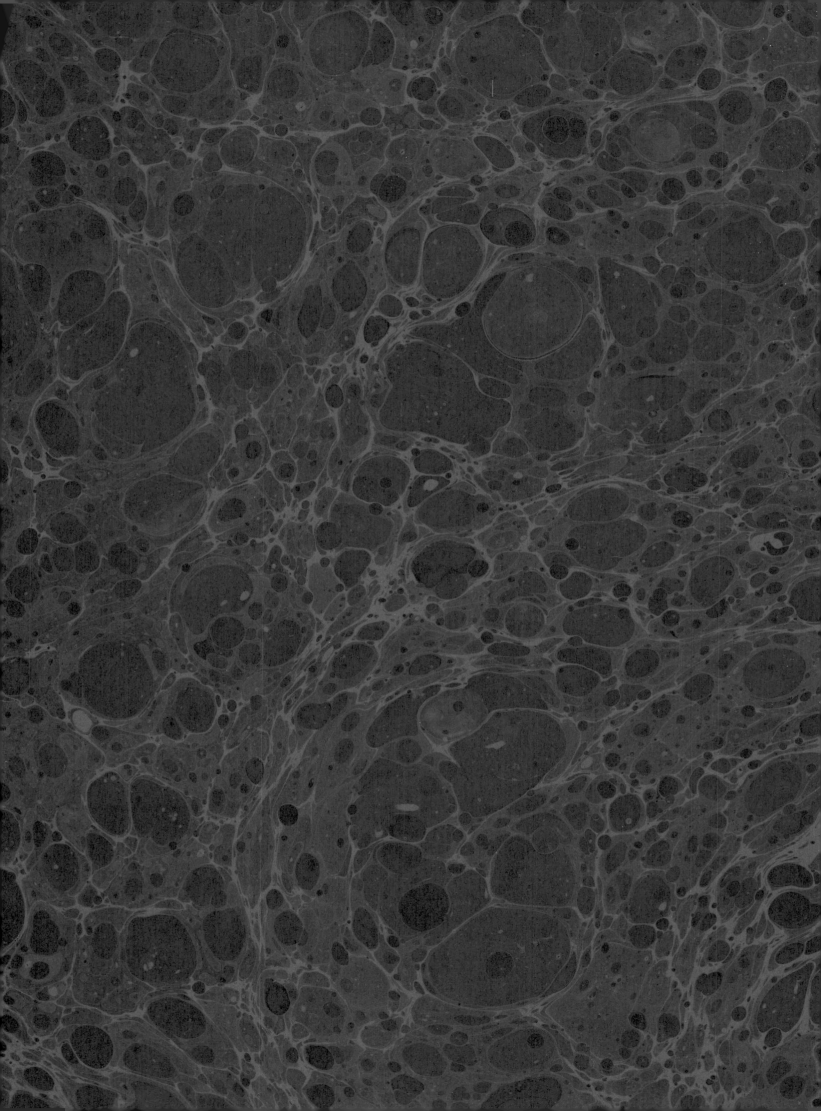